FROM
BEAR DENS
TO THE
Oval Office

True stories from my 38 years managing national parks.

SHERIDAN STEELE

CONTENTS

NPS MISSION: The National Park Service preserves unimpaired the natural and cultural resources and values of the National Park System for the enjoyment, education, and inspiration of this and future generations.

THE ORGANIC ACT OF 1916

The National Park Service Organic Act (16 U.S.C. 1 2 3, and 4), as set forth herein, consists of the Act of Aug. 25 1916 (39 Stat. 535) and amendments thereto.

Be it enacted by the Senate and House of Representatives of the United States of America in Congress assembled, That there is hereby created in the Department of the Interior a service to be called the National Park Service, which shall be under the charge of a director, who shall be appointed by the Secretary and who shall receive a salary of $4,500 per annum. There shall also be appointed by the Secretary the following assistants and other employees at the salaries designated: One assistant director, at $2,500 per annum, one chief clerk, at $2,000 per annum; one draftsman, at $1,800 per annum; one messenger, at $600 per annum; and, in addition thereto, such other employees as the Secretary of the Interior shall deem necessary. The service thus established shall promote and regulate the use of the Federal areas known as national parks, monuments, and reservations ...which purpose is to conserve the scenery and the natural and historic objects and the wild life therein and to provide for the enjoyment of the same in such manner and by such means as will leave them unimpaired for the enjoyment of future generations.

CHAPTER ONE

GROWING UP CAMPING

I often went to school with shirts that had ragged rips across the front and back. I told everyone that the parallel tears were from a bear's claws, which was true. Fortunately, I was not wearing the shirt at the time. In fact, those same rips were in all my shirts until my mother fixed them with iron-on patches. Let me explain.

As we drove through the gate to Yellowstone National Park, the ranger said, "We are warning everyone to avoid keeping food in your car or tent. The bears' natural food supply is scarce this summer, so they are looking for food in campsites." I was in the fourth grade and had camped with the family in various national parks over the past several summers. As we drove to the campground, we talked about which food of ours might attract bears and where to keep it.

As we set up our camp, we were careful not to put food in our tent or the car as the ranger warned. However, my dad had placed a cantaloupe in a metal container and put it in the canvas topped trailer we pulled to transport all our camping equipment. We still needed a luggage carrier on top of the car to carry the additional luggage, which left room inside the car for the four kids. Given all that stuff we were hauling with us, people often asked if we were moving. We would cheerfully reply that no, we were camping throughout the West. On that evening in our Yellowstone campsite, my dad put the garment bag over the top of the metal box confident the bears would not smell the cantaloupe underneath.

With two brothers and a sister, our family sized canvas tent was crowded so I volunteered to sleep in the back of our station wagon where I enjoyed the extra space. Something woke me up that first night and I looked out of the car windows to see a large bear on top of our canvas top trailer. The bear was ripping through the top and then the garment bag trying to find the cantaloupe. It turns out experts say that bears have the best sense of smell of any animal alive. The average dog's sense of smell is at least 100 times better than our human noses, but these animal experts say the bear's sense of smell is twenty times better than a dog, or 2,000 times better than us. In short, there is no hiding a juicy cantaloupe from a hungry bear.

We had a big plug-in spotlight in our car, and I used it to shine the strong beam into the bear's eyes. I kept flashing it back and forth until he jumped down and left but not before he had ripped right through the clothes in the garment bag, including all my shirts. The bear left before he reached the metal container but damage to our clothes was certainly not worth an eighty-nine cent cantaloupe.

My dad was a consulting engineer and we often took long trips from Ohio to the western states. We would camp in many state and national parks along the way and he would combine business with pleasure. Over the course of several of these cross-country trips, I fell in love with Colorado's Rocky Mountain National Park in particular and all national parks in general. I also particularly liked the arid and sunny climate of the Southwest.

– – – – – –

It never dawned on me that I could make a career out of working in the parks until I had graduated college and returned for a master's degree. In preparing to begin graduate school at Ohio State in urban and regional planning, I was looking at the list of required courses and other electives if I had the time. The courses that really caught my attention were subjects like wildlife management, park design, environmental engineering, and similar natural resource courses. These were not a good match for the Urban Planning Department where I was about to begin my graduate work. After this epiphany, I was fortunate to transfer to the School of Natural Resources and after two years of more stimulating course work, I earned my master's degree in natural resources management rather than urban planning. My undergraduate degree in business administration with a minor in public relations turned out to be a useful combination.

- - - - - -

As a lifelong camper, I have enjoyed camping in national and state parks where the natural environment was the attraction rather than the amenities found in commercial campgrounds such as KOA. I love the outdoors, especially the high mountain lakes surrounded by summer snowfields, the clear, dark night skies with millions of stars that are best seen out West, cascading mountain streams, the spray from huge waterfalls, and seeing wildlife in their natural habitat. It is a special thrill to see the newborns in early summer. I also love clean water and fresh air and sitting around a campfire having family conversations without electronics, bright lights, and other modern distractions.

- - - - - -

I always assumed I would marry someone who loved the outdoors as much as I did, and we would raise our family to enjoy camping, hiking, and the natural environment, and of course, national parks. In college, a group of friends and I would often go camping on weekends, and sometimes river rafting, canoeing, or bike riding. I remember having a VW Beetle, and every empty space would be full of camping gear, food, and drinks for our weekend trips.

My steady girlfriend during graduate school, Barb, told me she loved to camp and be in the outdoors as much as me, even being a good sport when sleeping through a downpour or packing up our wet tent and gear. Soon after we were married, her younger sister told me that her love of the outdoors was a "bit of a stretch," indicating that the only camping she had done before college

3

was one night with the Girl Scouts. However, we were married in an outdoor garden wedding and honeymooned in New England, exploring state and national parks but staying in hotels or cabins.

One memorable hotel was on Martha's Vineyard, an island off the coast of Massachusetts that required an hour's ferry ride each way. We stayed at an old inn in town that advertised a room with private entrance, ocean views, and balcony, and we reserved it thinking it was the perfect honeymoon choice. The brochure should have read: room with private entrance through the dining room, with a one-person balcony with ocean views only when the leaves are off the trees. Possibly the biggest surprise was the fact the room only had twin beds. We awoke to loud talking and the clanking of dishes from the dining room below. Since we could clearly make out the conversations below, we wondered what others could hear coming from the room above. Hardly a honeymoon suite!

We especially enjoyed a couple of days in Acadia National Park and Maine's large wilderness park named Baxter State Park in honor of Governor Percival Baxter. He had donated the land to the people of Maine. We were both impressed by the rugged beauty of Acadia and Maine, but neither of us would have ever guessed that I would someday come back as the park superintendent of Acadia. Having spent much of my career living in the West, Barb and I had agreed that Acadia was the only national park in the East that would entice us to move back. It turned out that my twelve years in Maine were some of the best times of my life and career.

- - - - - -

On one early road trip with Barb, we were camping in Glacier National Park in Montana, and she said, "Oh, I hope we get to see a bear. I really want to see a bear." Later that night, I awoke to breathing just outside the tent. I looked out the screened window and there was a black bear walking around our campsite. I woke up Barb and said, "You wanted to see a bear. Just look out the window." I was almost immediately back to sleep, and she shook me saying, "You can't go back to sleep. There is a bear out there!" We talked about the fact that our tent and campsite were clean, no food improperly stored, and the fact that black bears are not aggressive unless the female was protecting cubs. Therefore, the danger was minimal. She finally got back to sleep, which allowed me to finish the night in peace.

— — — — — —

After we married and before having children, we decided to take a four-month road trip through the western United States and Canada, camping most of the time. I took a leave of absence from my job at the Ohio Department of Natural Resources where I was a park planner, and we moved out of our apartment and stored our furniture in my parents' basement. Our 1973 Subaru station wagon was loaded to the gills with camping gear, clothing, and lots of stuff for all types of weather and activities.

We drove some 28,000 miles on that trip, and I took more than 2,000 color slides along the way. While that seemed like a lot to Barb, I told her it was only one every fourteen miles or so. To accurately label them when I got home, I kept a detailed log of photos taken each day. I mailed the exposed film to a Kodak processing lab and gave each mailer a number code to correspond to my photo log. All the slides were waiting for me to label when I returned home to my parents' house.

We left in early May from Columbus and headed to the Southwest where we thought the weather would be warmer. This allowed us to avoid the higher elevations where snow would still block many trails into the mountains and colder temperatures would not be conducive to tent camping. One of our first night's camping in Bryce Canyon National Park and guess what? It snowed several inches overnight. However, it was spectacular the next day with fresh snow on the red and orange hoodoos, as the colorful formations that make up Bryce are called. The result was many dramatic photos.

Because Bryce is 2,000 feet higher in elevation than nearby Zion National Park, we decided to move on to Zion, but not before we searched for any gear hidden by snow and packing our wet tent. Luckily, we found warmer temperatures and sunny days giving us several perfect days to explore Zion. We took several hikes, including one to Hidden Canyon where the trail climbs steeply before crossing a narrow ledge that leads to the isolated canyon. A chain hanging on the inside of the narrow ledge helped to provide a safe crossing. The ledge was more than 800 feet above our starting point, and we could see our tiny blue Subaru parked far below. One of our most memorable hikes was to Angels Landing in Zion. The two-and-a-half-mile trail climbs almost 1,500 feet to spectacular views of the Zion canyon far below. Beginning at the Grotto Trailhead, hikers follow the well-marked trail through Refrigerator Canyon, a cool respite from the sunny trail, and up the twenty-one switchbacks of Walter's Wiggles. It then climbs steeply up the ridge where chains and rails are provided in the most exposed areas. Once on top, it is easy to see why Angels Landing has become renowned for attracting hikers from around the world.

A few days later we drove to Grand Canyon, considered one of the Seven Wonders of the World. The immense and dramatic Grand Canyon is 277 miles long, eighteen miles wide and over a mile deep, making one feel small and insignificant indeed. I had made reservations to take the mule ride to the bottom and spend the night at Phantom Ranch on the Colorado River far below the rim. The day before we were to go early the following morning, Barb started getting nervous about being up high on trails and looking over the edge as the mules walked slowly down into the canyon. Seeking an expert opinion, I approached a friendly ranger and asked about the mule trip, telling him that my wife was afraid of heights. He suggested that if we really wanted to go, we should get on with everyone else and then it would be too late to back out; not the best advice as it turned out.

The next morning Barb was shocked to see that the mules were really big animals and not the little donkeys where your feet almost touched the ground, as she had imagined. Instead, she would be perched high off the ground on the back of a moving animal. She immediately headed to the restroom with a case of nervous stomach, so I took the opportunity to speak to the wrangler about her fears. He offered to place us together in line, one after the other, so I could talk to her on the four-hour ride down. They had us all mount up, and then we were divided into groups of men and women. All women went first, then the men. As promised, they put Barb as the last woman and me as the first man, so we were together in the group of about twenty riders.

In our late twenties, we seemed to be the only ones with dark hair, and everyone else seemed much older. Once ready to begin, the wrangler said we would ride down to the first major turn, pull off the trail, and have a group photo taken. We were instructed that anytime the mules stopped on the trail, we had to turn them so their heads were facing over the edge. That way they could see the edge and would not back off the cliff. At this point, Barb said loudly, "I don't like this!"

At the group photo spot, she said, "I am not going." She got off her mule exclaiming, "I can't do it, no way!" Of course, I dismounted and instead of consoling her, I quickly walked uphill to get a great photo of all of the mules and riders posing with the canyon behind and two empty saddles in the middle of the group. The wrangler told us there were no refunds, but I could tell that made no difference to normally frugal Barb. One wrangler took the two empty mules back to the livery, and Barb and I rode the park buses along the rim instead of the mules into the canyon. That day seemed to get worse when I left an expensive camera lens on one of the many shuttle buses making stops along the rim drive. Barb, feeling somewhat responsible for our change in plans, offered to get on the next bus hoping to catch up at some point. Fortunately, someone turned it in to the main bus terminal where I found it later that day.

Grand Canyon -Two mules without riders after my wife refused to go.

— — — — — —

Driving up to the entrance station at Yellowstone National Park as our trip was nearing its end, there was my name prominently listed on the emergency message board next to the ranger's window.

We immediately thought of a medical emergency or death in the family. We were relieved when we were handed a written message that read, "Please call Don at the Ohio Department of Natural Resources." Wondering what would prompt my boss to track us down, we found a pay phone (back in the day) and I called him.

Don asked if we were enjoying our trip visiting national parks of the West, and of course, I gave an enthusiastic response. He suggested we "might as well extend our trip" since there was a major state budget cut that would dramatically reduce the number of state workers, including many at the Department of Natural Resources. He said it was highly likely I would be among those laid off or terminated to save money. Since we had visited most of our planned places, we decided to return to Ohio, then strike off to New England for another month at peak fall color.

CHAPTER TWO

THE BEGINNING OF MY NATIONAL PARK CAREER

Cuyahoga Valley National Recreation Area, Management Assistant, 1978-1982

There is something to be said for "being in the right place at the right time". After graduating college with degrees in business administration and natural resources management, I began my professional career as a state park planner with the Ohio Department of Natural Resources. When that job evaporated due to budget cuts in state government, I took the Executive Director position for a private nonprofit called the Cuyahoga Valley Park Federation, in northern Ohio. Today, it probably would be called "Friends of the Cuyahoga Valley" or something like that, since its role was similar to Friends of Acadia and other such park support groups. One major difference, however, was that the Park Federation was an umbrella organization that had eighty-two different affiliates originally formed to advocate for preservation of the Cuyahoga Valley. Once Congress passed legislation that established the new recreation area in 1974, the Park Federation hired me to work in collaboration with the National Park Service as it began planning and acquisition for the new recreation area between Akron and Cleveland.

One of the eighty-two affiliates was the Cleveland Metroparks. When Barb and I moved to the Cleveland area from Columbus, the director of Metroparks offered to rent us one of the district's vacant houses on Metropark land. Thinking that living in a more rural park setting and in a less expensive rental house sounded like a good idea, we asked to look at one of the possible rentals. We preferred living near my new office in Peninsula, a small town surrounded by the national recreation area. We arranged to meet a park ranger at the specified house location to get a walk-through of the property. Following the ranger through a wooded setting to the house, we parked in the driveway. As we climbed the stairs to the front door, the ranger pulled out the key and his gun. I asked why he was entering the house with his gun out and his reply shocked us. "This house has become a real problem place with lots of drinking and other party type activity," he said. After seeing the fearful look on my wife's face, I told the ranger I didn't think this house would work for us, and we cut the tour short.

We rented a small apartment not far from Peninsula until we found a house to buy in nearby Hudson. The mostly white houses with black shutters gave Hudson the appearance of a small New England town, complete with an open town square surrounded by small shops and several churches with beautiful spires.

As executive director of the Cuyahoga Valley Park Federation, my responsibilities included working with the news media, public speaking, and enlisting volunteers to help achieve various organization goals established by our board of directors. I also became the unofficial park photographer since the NPS staff was limited in those start-up years. The official park staff began with a superintendent, secretary and one park ranger. There were many demands for photographs of the scenic beauty of the valley, various recreational uses, and partner attractions (such as the Metroparks and the historic Hale Farm) to use in public presentations, brochures, and other park-related materials.

To build our photo inventory quickly, I most often used my wife as a model doing something active, such as hiking or paddling a canoe but not facing the camera. For variety, Barb would take more than one color of blouse or jacket and change frequently to appear to be different people. Despite these efforts, after slide presentations, I would still get an occasional question about the woman who appeared in many of my photos.

Once I was looking for park users to photograph while enjoying the new park, and I approached a couple who had just driven up in separate cars. I asked if I could photograph them at the viewpoint. As they gave each other a frightened look, they politely declined and hurried off. I do not think they were supposed to be there, at least together.

Historic Wilson's Mill and the Ohio and Erie Canal.

Along Tinkers Creek, Cuyahoga Valley National Recreation Area (CVNRA).

— — — — — —

After a few years at the Park Federation and working alongside the first superintendent for Cuyahoga Valley, Bill Birdsell, the National Park Service was adding staff. The superintendent offered me a job doing the same types of things I had been doing for the Federation. Working for the National Park Service (NPS) had always been a dream job in my mind, so I eagerly jumped at this opportunity. Thinking of all those wonderful camping trips as a child, I hoped getting into the National Park Service would lead to a future job in one of the great western parks. My title at Cuyahoga was management assistant working directly for the superintendent and helping with planning, land acquisition, and public information.

The startup of a new national park in the rural area between two large cities had great public support except from those residents potentially most affected by acquisition of land for the new park. Various public meetings could become stressful situations because of the many questions, most without adequate answers since the planning effort was just getting underway. I often gave public presentations trying to explain NPS policies and priorities. I answered many difficult questions and tried to tamp down the numerous rumors that seemed to routinely spread through the valley.

One friendly audience was the Akron Isaac Walton League, a group of fishermen who seemed to be well into retirement, with the youngest person in the room probably seventy years. I was introduced after lunch and began my typical thirty-minute slide show. Within a few minutes of the lights going off, I heard one person snoring. By about ten minutes into the program, there were multiple people asleep and I was beginning to wonder if there was anyone still awake. I had to assume someone was listening, so I continued. I prefer to think it was a combination of the lunch, time of day, and age of the group rather than the program content or quality of the speaker. At the end of the program, I pretty much shouted for someone to turn on the lights and said in a loud voice I would answer questions. Since most had slept through the program, there were few questions asked.

Cuyahoga tended to generate controversy, especially locally in the small town of Peninsula, named from the landform on the Cuyahoga River. Area landowners were concerned about which private parcels would be acquired and what that meant for residences in the valley. This resulted in some strong emotions at any public meeting when local landowners were present. I spoke at several of those meetings and often showed slides that illustrated why the Cuyahoga Valley was significant as a national park and what it would likely become over time. Since the law that established the park had specific provisions related to acquiring properties and since landowners were anxious to learn how it would affect them, I tried to answer their questions. It got heated at times, even after people were assured that the law allowed residential owners to delay acquisition. Landowners were told that our highest priority was to buy the undeveloped parcels to protect the rural character of the valley, but mistrust persisted. The law provided for homeowners to retain title to the land if they agreed to some restrictions limiting further development. As an option, they could sell their property to the park but remain living there through their own lifetime (called "life estate").

We made some mistakes in the early years of land acquisition. There was one family business that sold topsoil that naturally accumulated on the flood plains of the Cuyahoga River. The decision was made to acquire that land to end the practice of scraping the rich soil into piles and then selling it for residential purposes all over northeastern Ohio. A ruling was made that any of the existing piles of soil available for sale must be purchased at market value or what people would pay by the truckload. The family owners quickly amassed huge piles of topsoil, probably enough for several years of future sales, and the government paid a large sum of money to purchase that property. A more serious mistake was not buying other flood plain parcels along the river *before* we ended the family topsoil business. Being smart business people, that family used the great profit from our first purchase to buy as much other flood plain land as possible in order to scrape many more tall piles of topsoil to be sold to the government at truckload prices. Their market suddenly vastly improved as did sales, and we soon saw members of the family driving around in new pickups and Cadillacs.

We also bought an abandoned farm property that had several ravines full of junk that turned out to be hundreds of drums of waste oil and other chemicals hidden under surface debris. The cost of cleanup was a significant unwelcome surprise. In fact, the extensive cleanup took years and cost so much that the policy was changed, whereas future acquisitions required a pre-purchase survey to ensure no toxic waste was on the land. Lesson learned!

– – – – – –

Using volunteers, we offered group tours that highlighted the historic and scenic features of the valley to build public support for the developing park. We also published a colorful free poster that had a collage of sixteen images of the scenic features and recreational uses illustrating all four seasons. The poster had the title "Cuyahoga Valley, For All People, For All Time" to convey the message of its present and future potential for all Americans and to counter the negative publicity from unhappy landowners. One thing I learned about the news media is that even if 95 percent of the public support something like a new park and 5 percent oppose the plan, both sides are treated either as equals or the opposing side gets the (negative) headline. It seemed "good news doesn't sell newspapers" was true.

Part of my public affairs role with the National Park Service was to deal regularly with the news media. One day I agreed to meet with the Cleveland Plain Dealer investigative reporter who I was sure was going to focus on the land controversy. Knowing it could have the potential of being negative and one-sided, I asked to meet her at one of the park's scenic overlooks where we could begin on a positive note. I then offered to give her a tour while we talked, and she agreed. She preferred to drive, so I locked my car and got in with her.

The tour and my responses to her many questions went well. Upon returning to the parking lot some ninety minutes later, I got out of her car and instinctively reached for my car key. When it was not in my pocket, I instantly knew I had locked it in the Park Service car, complete with the NPS logo on the door. Rather than admit that to her, for fear she might include some mention of it in her article, I told her I was going back to the overlook before leaving, and she drove off. So, there I was, in the park ranger uniform and flat hat, locked out of my car, and no radio or other way to quietly get help. It was spring and few other people were in the park, so I walked about a quarter mile to the nearest house and knocked on the door. A woman approached and seeing this uniformed ranger at her door, she opened up and I said, "Excuse me ma'am, but someone has locked their keys in their car down the road, and I would like to help them. Do you have a coat hanger I could have?" Once provided, I walked back to the car, and I was able to open the car through the window gap. It wouldn't be so easy with today's electric locks.

— — — — — —

The new national recreation area incorporated several existing metropolitan parks (regional parks) that were to be turned over to the NPS at some point. Understandably, the two park districts (Akron and Cleveland) were not anxious to give up their long-held park units, and they delayed as long as possible. Virginia Kendall Park, with beautiful facilities built by the Civilian

Conservation Corps (CCC), even had an operating endowment that went with the land, which made the Akron Metropolitan Parks reluctant to transfer Kendall. However, the law establishing the national recreation area mandated that Virginia Kendall be immediately conveyed. That particularly upset the Akron Metro District because they depended on the endowment to fund a large part of their own operation, including some of their other parks.

Among the CCC facilities, now considered historic for their distinctive qualities, were the beautiful Octagon Shelter picnic facility, Happy Days Shelter, and a unique wooden toboggan chute. Like the eight-sided picnic shelter called the Octagon, the beautiful rustic shelter buildings had great stone fireplaces and other unique design features.

The wooden toboggan chute was several hundred feet long and had two drops in its length, allowing sleds to go nearly forty miles per hour under the right conditions. The chutes were iced down by spraying water on the wooden planks and side walls. People borrowed toboggans from the warming house below, walked up the torch-lit path to the top and waited for their turn. The chutes ended at the Kendall Lake surface, so the ice had to be at least nine inches thick before the toboggan run was opened.

On the first night of operation by the National Park Service, we decided to have a dress rehearsal to make sure we knew how things should go. We invited the news media, park employees, and volunteers to come for the trial run. Someone remembered when Akron Metro operated the toboggan run, workers would sweep the lake surface to remove snow that slowed the sleds prematurely. However, we didn't do enough research and learned the hard way that you shouldn't sweep all away across the lake. Some of the lake surface had to remain snow covered to slow the sleds to a stop before hitting the bank on the other side.

Because I was the park person responsible for dealing with the media, I was on the first toboggan sled down the chute with a TV cameraman and a reporter. It was a thrilling ride down the two levels and onto the ice. We were going fast enough that without some snow on the lake surface, we kept much of our speed all the way across until we hit the bank on the other side. It made for great television coverage since the cameraman caught all the action, including the sudden stop, on camera. Crews were soon sweeping snow back over some of the ice toward the end of the run to provide the essential braking action.

Twin toboggan chutes built by Civilian Conservation Corps.

The second superintendent, Lou Albert, came to Cuyahoga in 1981 after the sudden death of Bill Birdsell. With this change in leadership, it was a good time to look for other positions in the National Park Service for which I might apply and transfer if selected. The position vacancies at all national parks were listed internally, and any qualified NPS employee could apply. Most people had their own individual criteria for parks they might be interested in, and they applied it when checking the National Park Service vacant job lists. It was up to each person to research the parks and communities where one might wish to apply. With young children, the quality of local schools was important to us. In addition, I would inquire about other quality-of-life issues and any notable park challenges. No one liked to take a new job only to be surprised by a major challenge. My wife and I favored small towns where safety and security were typically not problems. Except for one year in Washington, D. C., we stayed in small towns for my entire career.

Fortunately, after three years at Cuyahoga, I was selected for my first super-intendence at Fort Scott National Historic Site in Kansas. I never thought I would live and work in Kansas, especially in the National Park Service. Competition for NPS jobs is always keen for the most popular spots like Grand Canyon, Yellowstone or Yosemite, so the best way to move up in the organization is to find a lesser known park where there will be fewer applicants for jobs. Fort Scott was such a place since it had only been added to the National Park System a few years earlier. It was pretty much an unknown park, and besides, it was in Kansas after all.

My strategy paid off, and I accepted the superintendent's position at Fort Scott NHS. The National Park Service normally allows four to six weeks to make the move to a new position in another park. Being our first move with kids old enough to possibly feel uprooted, Barb and I talked about our approach to breaking the news to Chris, five, and Kelly, three. We decided the best way was to explain why we were moving and tell them about the positive things in the new town in Kansas. Kelly was not old enough to understand the need for a career move or what it might mean to her. Chris on the other hand, did have some young friends he would have to leave behind. So, we approached the discussion carefully and thoughtfully. After a somewhat lengthy explanation by both Barb and me, we asked Chris, "So what do you think?" Very seriously, he asked, "Do they have pizza there?" Of course, the answer was yes. That was the end of the discussion as far as Chris was concerned, and he seemed satisfied that if they had pizza in Kansas, everything would be okay.

Being our first official transfer, the packing and moving of household goods (furniture, clothing, and more) was paid by the government. We learned a lot in that move. For instance, the more boxes the packers used the more money they made. Therefore, as we unpacked at the other end, we found boxes that only had one item in them, another box that had empty pizza boxes and trash (evidently remains of the packers' lunch). One box contained a tea kettle full of water, although the water was now throughout the packing material in the box. Packers worked quickly, and they could pack everything from a large house in one day. We also learned what things should be separated from the packing because they would be needed before boxes were unpacked on the other end (such as toiletries, medicines, pillows, and bedding) or valuables that needed to be handled carefully or protected from potential loss. For example, we didn't discover until weeks later that a number of valuable silver dollars did not get packed, and it was not possible to make a claim without proof. We knew we would plan ahead next time, setting aside in a well-marked pile those items we would move ourselves. One friend advised us to put those things in the bathtub where they wouldn't be confused with nearby items to be packed. On the other end, movers would unload everything, set up beds, and then leave all the other unpacking to us. It was usually a few weeks before we could get rid of the last of the boxes and packing material.

CHAPTER THREE
MOVING WEST

Fort Scott National Historic Site, Superintendent 1982-1988

T he lightning bolt struck in the middle of the night. Fortunately, all of the buildings on the fort grounds had rooftop lightning rods because of frequent severe thunderstorms, but this strike could have started a fire. The lightning rods were connected to metal cables that ran down the sides of the buildings and into a long metal stake in the ground. This technique works well if there is no metal path to somewhere other than the ground stake. We learned this the hard way. Someone had inadvertently driven a long spike through the wall that touched the cable running down the building exterior from the lightning rod on the roof. The lightning bolt hit that rod and traveled down the cable and then along the spike, exiting in an office. The next morning, the occupant of that office found numerous holes in the plaster around the spike and hundreds of small burn marks on the papers on the desktop. We were fortunate that a fire had not started and destroyed the historic building or multiple buildings. Of course, the threat of fire was even more frightening back in the 1840s when there was no equipment, adequate water, or trained firefighters available.

- - - - - -

"The Permanent Indian Frontier" didn't last long. The popular concept of that time was that Indian Territory would remain west of Missouri's western boundary, and a string of military forts, like Fort Scott, would assure the separation of Native Americans from settlers. The gold rush in California and the pressure to push homesteading west soon made the concept obsolete.

Fort Scott, named for General Winfield Scott, was built in 1842 on a bluff overlooking the Marmaton River. Both dragoons, the forerunners of the cavalry, and infantry were stationed at the fort which had a hospital, grand officers' quarters, an eighty-stall horse stable, enlisted barracks, guard house, and quartermaster's warehouse facing the parade ground. Captain Thomas Swords oversaw construction and then died from an accidental gunshot wound suffered on the parade ground.

Author's wife and daughter participate in costumed interpretation
on the parade ground at Fort Scott National Historic Site.

Volunteers dressed as dragoons outside the officers' quarters.

The sixteen surviving buildings, including some reconstructed buildings that made up the historic fort, became Fort Scott National Historic Site in 1978 by an act of Congress. The new site, managed by the National Park Service, soon had staff. In 1982, I was named the second superintendent following Glen Clark who took a job in the Washington office.

– – – – – –

I wondered how someone in the local grocery store knew who I was and where I lived after a man inside said, "Hey, I like your new fence." Fort Scott was my first real experience living in a small town (population 9,000), and I was surprised how everyone seemed to know everybody and everything. As the new superintendent of Fort Scott, my picture had been on the front page of the paper, and word of mouth let people know we had bought the gray house at the corner of 12th and National, the main street. We quickly put up the wooden fence to keep our two small children from wandering onto National Avenue, the busiest street in town. Another thing people noticed was when Barb began decorating a corner of our front porch for each season. We occasionally heard comments from complete strangers about the decorations and her changes from time to time.

Small town life is personal, particularly when you occupy a high-profile position like superintendent of the national historic site. It is like the saying, being a "big fish in a small sea." The "old fort," as locals called it, was important both due to the history of the town and as a tourist draw, giving a significant boost to the economy. Units of the National Park System were of particular interest to travelers, so various highway maps identified these sites – and tourists came to town.

Fort Scott had only one telephone exchange, so when you gave your phone number you only needed to say the last four digits. Of course, this was before fax machines and mobile phones. Back then, families only had the house phone (sounds like ancient history now). There was also an element of trust compared to life in the big city. Having moved from the Cleveland urban area, I was surprised when local merchants didn't ask for identification to cash a check. Once before grocery stores took credit cards, I forgot my checkbook after having filled my shopping cart with groceries at Ed's IGA. Ed had rung it up, and he told me to take the groceries home and come back with a check later that day or the next. He put my name on the receipt and put it in the cash drawer. Barb and I also learned the hard way that while shopping at Ed's grocery, you needed to hold on to your cart at all times. The old wooden floors were uneven, and your cart would roll away from you until it was stopped by the nearest display, cans, or jars on the shelves across the aisle.

– – – – – –

I have many small-town stories, but my favorite was when Tim Emerson (who soon became a friend of ours) moved from New York City to Fort Scott to take over the area's largest longhorn cattle ranch. He had been a stockbroker (not livestock) and his wife, Ann, was in advertising, but they decided they wanted to raise their two young boys in a friendlier and safer environment. He applied for the ranch manager position and several other advertised jobs in small towns so they could leave New York City behind. Soon after moving to town, he went to the one and only hardware to get a pocket knife, a necessity for any rancher. The owner met him at the door just as he did for any customer, and Tim introduced himself as the new ranch manager. The owner asked Tim what he was shopping for, and Tim told him he needed a pocket knife. "The cheapest one you have since I'll likely lose it before long," he said. The owner showed Tim to his knife case and pulled out his best knife, saying that if Tim bought his best one, he wouldn't lose it. Tim argued for the cheapest one until finally the owner insisted he take his most expensive one as a welcome gift. As Tim was leaving, the owner said, "I am sure you won't lose it." Tim took the knife home and put it in his sock drawer, never to use it because, as suspected, each time he went into the hardware the owner asked him if he still had that knife. When Tim said yes, the owner would say, "See, I told you so," For everyday use, Tim had purchased a cheaper knife from another store in a nearby town.

Tim, or rather his truck, made the front page of the local paper one day the following spring. He had a sick calf that he was bringing to the local vet. It was cold so Tim put the calf in the front seat of his truck and turned the heat on. He made a quick stop at the Quick Trip for coffee and let the engine run to keep the calf warm. While Tim was inside, the calf evidently bumped the gear shift, which caused the truck to roll back into the main street and hit a light pole on the other side. Fortunately, there were no injuries and little damage, so there was no need to cite the calf for driving without a license.

Needing some shelf brackets for a closet project, I went to the same town hardware store. The owner asked what I needed, I told him, and he escorted me to the proper bin. He asked how many I needed, and I replied "six." I thought I was in luck because there were six in the bin, but the owner said, "Sorry, I can't sell you all six, but I could let you have four." When I asked why not, he said, "Well, I wouldn't have any left in case someone else needs some brackets." I thought that was somewhat odd logic. I had to wait for his next shipment to come in. This was the same laid-back hardware that often had a small musical jam session in the back at lunch time. While customers might have to wait to get the owner's attention, at least they could enjoy the music.

— — — — —

Our old farmhouse on the main street had a nice two-sided porch with a hanging swing. Barb and I would sit out there on summer evenings to watch the heavy traffic on National Avenue. After only a couple of nights, we began to see the same cars over and over. It didn't take long to figure out that these were mostly high school kids making repeat trips between the local Sonic Drive-In and the Quick Trip, a distance of about one mile. It was not a matter of boredom, but rather a desire to be seen in one's car. Another unusual thing about teenagers driving in Kansas was that farm kids could drive at age fourteen but only if needed to get to school or jobs in town. However, this law was widely ignored, and some parents bought cars for their young drivers.

— — — — —

Meanwhile, with a small permanent staff and budget, we had to be as efficient as possible at the historic site. We combined the visitor center and bookstore functions into one building and recruited more volunteers to help augment the staff. The reconstructed hospital building became our visitor center with a small viewing room for a slideshow orientation program. The building's upstairs was furnished like the hospital used to be. Mostly visitors took self-guided tours around the site with the aid of a map and printed guide developed for the purpose. The primary rooms in each building had wall-mounted exhibit panels with an artist's rendering of a typical scene and brief text to explain the historic uses of those rooms.

— — — — —

The Harpers Ferry Center in West Virginia had historical architects, historians, and craftsmen such as woodcarvers, painters, and media specialists who could lend their expertise to the park as needed for projects. They would help develop interpretive exhibits, do research, and even write brochures and other handout materials. They provided the text for the exhibit panels at Fort Scott and also produced the primary park brochure. As one example of their services, we submitted paint and wallpaper samples from the historic buildings to determine the original paint colors and wallpaper from the 1840 time period. They could have replica wallpaper made where it was needed. Historians from the Harpers Ferry Center were also tasked with buying furniture and furnishings appropriate to the time period according to a carefully researched furnishings plan.

When the large semi tractor-trailer pulled up in front of the historic site, it was like Christmas with hundreds of presents to unwrap. The truck was full of antique furniture and furnishings appropriate to the time period that would fill the empty rooms at the fort. Each item was carefully wrapped and destined for one of the thirty-three rooms. From now on, visitors would walk through the buildings and get a better understanding of what life was like in the 1840s in a remote frontier outpost.

One of 33 furnished rooms in the historic site.

Baking bread in the bakehouse.

In addition to furnishings, we made other changes to improve the visitor experience at this 1842 frontier fort. Modern elements in and around the fort needed to be removed or hidden. For example, fire hydrants were hidden under wooden barrels with the word "water" stenciled on them, stacks of firewood were placed around modern heat pumps outside, and pictures were placed in front of thermostats. A replica thirty-star flag flew over the parade ground, and a recording of bugle calls played at the appropriate times. The authentic smells inside the stables came from the occasional horse or two that would be placed in stalls, to the delight of visitors. A rope prevented people from getting too close.

- - - - - -

Being a new unit of the National Park System, Fort Scott National Historic Site was obviously not yet marked on all road maps, and it was barely known even in the region. I thought it would be good to increase publicity related to the site so more visitors would come, and tourism would become an important element of the local economy. It was easier to enlist local cooperation in protecting significant natural or cultural resources once the benefits of tourism became obvious. However, to increase tourism, we needed to develop some colorful public programs to attract area travelers and visitors from nearby towns and cities. We started planning some major special events and routine interpretive (educational) programs that visitors would enjoy. We began publicizing four special events to present annually on specific weekends and a range of other daily activities related to the history of the fort.

One of the special events was the Dragoon (mounted horse soldiers) and Infantry Encampment, where re-enactors camped in canvas tents on the grounds for the weekend and lived as if they were in the 1840s. Re-enactors are organized groups of experienced hobbyists who have carefully studied life in the time period with special interest in the military history. They wore accurate reproduction (replica) uniforms and other clothing, and they used reproduction equipment such as firearms, horse tack, and other items appropriate to the time period. They ate and slept in circles of tents with the dragoons not mixing with the infantry because of a natural rivalry.

Photo on previous page: Reenactors dressed as Infantry during a weekend encampment. Photo above: Dragoons with 1842 "wrist breaker" sabers preparing to practice "Running at the Heads" drill.

Dragoon and infantry soldiers took turns on guard duty through the night by walking around the perimeter of the fort grounds in and out of the restored tallgrass prairie areas. I remember one of these weekend events when sometime after 2 a.m., an infantry soldier heard noise coming from the tallgrass and thought it might be a dragoon ready to play a trick. He lowered his rifle and challenged the unseen intruder. Out of the grass sprung up a naked man and woman with hands held high, and they yelled, "Don't shoot, don't shoot!" It seems they had closed one of the nearby local bars and were looking for a quiet place where they wouldn't be disturbed – "looking for love in all the wrong places."

– – – – – –

Historically, there were as many as eighty horses in the stables and each company of dragoons would have a designated color of horse to allow easy identification in the field. Company D had "blacks" while Company A rode "chestnuts."

All national parks use volunteers to augment staff and help serve visitors in a variety of ways, but I think Fort Scott is the only park that had "volunteer horses." Since the dragoons were horse soldiers, and the long stable building was an important interpretive exhibit, we decided the visitor experience would be greatly enhanced if there were at least a few horses in the stables during heavy visitor periods. Volunteers with horses would leave them in the stables for events or for a busy weekend just for the ambiance. Visitors were delighted when they entered the stables, and they heard and smelled the horses. Sometimes visitors could interact with a dragoon in uniform doing stable duties or working on tack. Visitors were favorably impressed, and the volunteers liked being the center of attention too. Sometimes fully dressed and equipped volunteer dragoons would ride their horses around the parade ground and pose for photos with visitors.

Historically, the dragoons participated in a practice called "running at the heads" where spherical-shaped objects were set on top of posts on the parade ground. Dragoons would ride their horse through the maze and swing their saber from side to side, trying to hit the target spheres. The replica 1840 military sabers were called "wrist breakers" because they were heavy and hard to use properly. One day, a volunteer dragoon was riding through the course attempting to hit the targets, and instead he somehow sliced the nose of his own horse. Fortunately for the horse, the rider was one of the local doctors. It was not a serious injury, but it took a few weeks before the horse was ready (and willing) to try "running at the heads" again.

One of my favorite events was the annual December Candlelight Tour. We had historically accurate vignettes staged around the fort, inside some of the buildings, and on the parade ground. Volunteers and staff were dressed in appropriate military uniforms or civilian attire. We had one dragoon ride a horse around the fort grounds just to add some color. He had no speaking part. There were almost 600 candle lanterns that lighted the way, and fires in fireplaces and candles inside the buildings for atmosphere and lighting. Otherwise it was dark, which added to the effect. Downtown Fort Scott was just a few hundred yards away, but we enlisted the community to help, not only as costumed volunteers, but by shutting off nearby street lights for the evening. The stage was set.

Hundreds of luminaries lined the parade ground for the candlelight tour.

Annual candlelight tour with more than 30 costumed
interpreters interacting with tour groups.

Volunteers and staff became the actors who talked about life in the military at an isolated frontier outpost while they interacted with each other and the touring public. The staff historian had provided reading material and sample scripts for the evening dialogue. Groups of ten to twelve left the visitor center every fifteen minutes, each with a costumed guide. The first group on the first night of the candlelight tours got a surprise. Wendell, dressed as a dragoon soldier, rode a borrowed horse slowly around the parade ground to the thrill of those on tour. He would appear from time to time up close or in the distance, which brought the fort to life for the evening. Suddenly Wendell's horse bolted, throwing him off, and temporarily knocking him out when he hit the ground. Many of the costumed volunteers sprang into action and worked to corner and calm the horse. Once safely in the stables, with Wendell up and walking, one person turned to their guide and exclaimed, "Wow, do you do that for every tour?" Fortunately, not.

The Candlelight Tour was a huge hit, and it is no wonder with twenty-five to thirty people in costume and eight to ten colorful vignettes staged around the fort. People toured the officers' quarters, the quartermaster's warehouse, the hospital, the mess hall (with fiddle music), the barracks, and the stables with a dozen or more horses in the stalls. Hearing the horses and smelling the hay in the stables made a real impression on people. The Candlelight Tour was sold out every year, and soon bus tours began coming especially for this unique and colorful event.

These special events were carefully planned interpretive experiences for visitors. In addition, on most summer days we would have one or more costumed interpreters staged around the site to talk about the history of the fort and life in the 1800s. Ranger Alice often dressed as an officer's wife and would stand by a crackling fire in the officer's quarters while Ranger Randy Kane would act and dress the part of an infantry sergeant. The National Park Service calls this interpretation, and others call it education. When it involves role playing of another time period, it was called living history. The goal was to make the experience of visiting these national park historic areas more meaningful by focusing on the history in ways that grabbed a visitor's attention and held their interest.

Alice was one of our best interpreters. A local woman who had never flown on an airplane, she was excited to be chosen to go to Bent's Fort, a national park site in Colorado, for a live-in weekend of training in the 1850 time period. Participants were to come prepared to play a role, either soldier, trader, or domestic, and learn from the experience as guided by experts in history of that time period. Alice chose domestic, which was cooking and other domestic duties of the time.

The man in charge of domestics' training led the small group of six women over to a corral of pigs. He pulled his handgun from his waist belt and fired, killing one pig. He announced it was time to fix supper for the troops. Fortunately, Alice had grown up on a local farm, and while not expecting that approach, she was able to complete the chores and lived to tell about it. Her only complaint was that domestics had to sleep on the wooden plank floor with a buffalo skin for a blanket.

– – – – – –

The replica uniforms, military equipment, and other period costumes were made possible by a local printer who donated a fundraising brochure called "Partners in Preservation." The one-page folded brochure highlighted all of the items we needed to develop a wide array of new 1840-1865 interpretive programs, including living history programs and special events. For example, the brochure listed reproduction dragoon uniforms at $275 each, three Grimsley saddles at $756 each, an 1842 horse pistol at $200, a thirty-star garrison flag at $450, and several 1840 "wrist-breaker" model cavalry sabers at $150 each. The two most expensive items were a replica twelve-pounder mountain howitzer (that would fire) at $7,000 and a U.S. quartermaster freight wagon at $15,000.

The park historian provided the oversight and guidance to be sure the purchased items were accurate reproductions. He researched and found the army's exact specifications from 1840 for a freight wagon at the Smithsonian Institution in Washington, D.C. Once we had lined up donated funding, we provided those specifications to a wagon maker in Ohio who produced a replica for use at the fort. It was an exciting day when the local trucking company brought the wagon from Ohio to Fort Scott. It became part of the permanent display at the quartermaster's building.

Top: Replica army freight wagon purchased using private donations. Bottom:
Cannon firing demonstration by park rangers dressed as Dragoons.

Back in 1983, park superintendents were permitted to be more active in
seeking private donations to accomplish projects that would otherwise languish.
I visited many local businesses and organizations to distribute the brochure
and talk about the potential for improving the fort's programs if we could
obtain these uniforms, replica equipment and accessories. The wildly success-

ful campaign raised nearly $100,000 in this small town, and we were able to purchase everything listed in the brochure.

Enthusiasm was high in the community for the expanded public programs, the new initiatives, and increased publicity to attract more visitors. In addition to the fundraising, we embarked on an effort to recruit local and regional volunteers who would help us develop a variety of new public interpretation programs. The Volunteers in Parks program at Fort Scott drew from surrounding communities and involved almost 300 people of all ages who were willing to study the history of the fort and time period and participate in interpretive programs and special events. Volunteers would help with annual events, daily tours, and activities, staffing of the visitor center desk, and otherwise support our growing public programming. It became the second largest volunteer program in the Midwest Region of the National Park Service. Not bad for a town of 9,000 people.

- - - - - -

Once, I received a 1:00 a.m. phone call from the local police department telling me someone was yelling for help from the fort's guard house, also known as the jail. The rangers were supposed to check each building before locking it up for the night, but in this case, someone was evidently back in a cell and missed by the ranger closing buildings. The man from Iowa explained that once he realized he was locked in he yelled for a ranger, but no one heard him. He then hoped he would see someone walking by but saw no one. As the hours rolled by, he got cold in the stone building with no comfortable furniture, so he began to yell for help. Fortunately, he took the experience with good humor and said he didn't expect to be jailed for not leaving the area on time.

- - - - - -

We had a talented maintenance staff at Fort Scott so building repairs and restoration work could be done to strict NPS professional standards. We also had a staff historian who researched the history of the fort and the time period.

Our entire professional staff numbered fifteen and we added three to five seasonal employees in the summer depending on the year's budget. Our extensive volunteer program enabled us to provide a wider range of interpretation and information services, which really meant the visitors to Fort Scott National Historic Site had a more meaningful experience. One of the historic officer's quarters was vacant, and no public use was contemplated. The interior was authentic, or what we call "historic fabric," original building components that have not been drastically changed over time. The interior of this building had some modern drywall in some places, but once that was removed the building components became a terrific display of building techniques used in the 1840s. The building framework was exposed, showing the mortice and tendon joints, hand hewn logs, and wooden pegs used in lieu of nails. Plastered walls were still original with a mix of horsehair and plaster. Wooden floors were eighteen- to twenty-four-inch wide planks, and the massive columns on the porches were solid black walnut with an airway through the middle. Even the clapboard siding was solid black walnut, and the dense nature of that wood has kept the original fabric in excellent condition for over 175 years. As a winter project, our craftsman made the building interior into an educational exhibit to be opened to the public. The building had no heat, so crews used a temporary portable construction heater to keep the uninsulated building around forty-five degrees to make work possible. One of the crew brought in a wall thermostat that would normally be used at home to regulate their furnace. They mounted it on the wall. When it seemed too cold, someone would say, "Hey, turn up the heat will you?" and another worker would turn up the thermostat just for a little levity. After several months, the result was an excellent exhibit on frontier building construction in the 1840s.

— — — — — —

Fort Scott National Historic Site gave me a great opportunity to become a park superintendent in the National Park System at an entry level. Subsequently, I took other superintendent positions in six different national park units over thirty-two years of my thirty-eight-year career. I enjoyed building a good team to accomplish important goals and resolving challenges that varied from park to park. Community relations were also a personal priority that helped increase public support and volunteerism. Peter Drucker, a well-known management authority, wrote that "management is doing things right" and "leadership is doing the right things." I enjoyed both roles, but I particularly liked the goal and priority setting by engaging both the park staff and the community. We accomplished many good things by working as a team and maintaining focus on "the right things."

Superintendents were loosely supervised by regional directors in another city. In the case of Fort Scott National Historic Site, the regional director was in Omaha, Nebraska. I would travel to Omaha two to three times per year to consult with regional office specialists (historic architects, engineers, personnel specialists, and others). On one visit a year I would meet with the regional director for my performance evaluation. Otherwise, we were fairly autonomous in the field at the various park units. I appreciated the opportunity to operate without a great deal of daily oversight.

Park units were not only spread out and remote, they usually were far from the political pressures of Washington. The director and regional directors had to work the politics on the national level while park superintendents were more involved with local politics and communications with state and local officials and other stakeholders.

— — — — — —

CHAPTER FOUR

A MANAGEMENT TRAINING YEAR IN WASHINGTON, DC

A fter seven rewarding years as superintendent at Fort Scott, I applied for a special Department of the Interior training opportunity called the Departmental Management Development Program (DMDP). The one-year program selected a single field manager each year to move to Washington, D.C., to learn how decisions, policies, and laws are made that directly affect the National Park Service. Many field managers applied for the prestigious, highly competitive DMDP. I had to apply for a second year before I made the final four, which meant I would be interviewed.

The director of the National Park Service at the time was William Penn Mott, who had been director of California State Parks for many years before he retired. In his early eighties, he was named NPS director by President Ronald Reagan. Director Mott wanted to personally select the field manager who would come to Washington for the year. The date was set for him to interview the four finalists for the program, which meant I would have to arrange travel to DC. My appointment with the director was for 1 p.m., and it would be just the two of us in his office. Much to my dismay, he fell asleep as I was answering his second question. I was hoping it was not the quality of my answer that put him to sleep, but the dilemma for me was what to do next. Rather than bump him to wake him up, I decided to continue my answer, but in an increasingly loud voice until I was almost yelling. His eyes slowly opened and we both acted as if nothing happened.

Although I thought the interview would have been better for me if he had not dozed off, I got the position and our family moved to Washington from Kansas for one year. The actual move turned out to be a memorable five-day drive from Fort Scott to suburban Washington. We had a miniature black dachshund named Samantha who had a peculiar habit. She hated windshield wipers, so when they were turned on, she would throw herself at the dashboard, growling and barking, trying to bite the wipers through the glass. We often said a video of her viciousness toward wipers would have made a great submission for America's Funniest Videos. It was hilarious, until just before our long drive East, when she injured her back and the local veterinarian recommended bed rest and confinement to a small portable dog bed. Thinking about driving through the Midwest in late spring brought to mind thunderstorms and long periods of rain. Samantha would not be still if we had to turn on the wipers, but we couldn't leave her behind. In desperation, I decided to try Rain-X, a liquid applied to glass that made the water "sheet off," allowing clearer vision without wipers – and it worked. Even though we experienced several storms on the five-day drive, Samantha remained calm throughout the trip.

Moving to Washington was an actual job transfer that meant my former job at Fort Scott would be occupied by a new superintendent, and I would have to compete for a new assignment when my training year ended. Not knowing where I might go after Washington was a concern to the whole family so there was some career risk involved. However, the development program was a prestigious accomplishment, and hopefully it would lead to another desirable park assignment. It was always possible to get stuck in Washington or in a less desirable park because of the timing of park position vacancies.

We rented a house in suburban Virginia, and I began to commute to work on the Metro train. It was quite a cultural shock for our two kids, now in fourth and sixth grades. Our son's middle school had students from around the world who spoke more than 25 different languages. On one family outing downtown, the kids were upset to learn about (and see) homeless people, but they also got to see the White House, Congress, and Supreme Court. This helped them to better understand our system of government.

Making the most of the year in our nation's capital, we
enjoyed the many free things to see and do.

My training program allowed me to design my own approach that would introduce me to various players in our nation's capital. The goal was to arrange temporary work assignments, called details, in Washington that would help me understand the larger picture of our organization and how it fit in the executive branch of government. In addition, I learned about the important role of the U.S. Congress, which has tremendous influence over our mission, funding, and legal framework. While I had guidance from NPS leadership, I had complete freedom to choose how to best spend my year in Washington.

The year was split into two different details: the first one was acting as an assistant to the National Park Service director, working on assignments where my field experience would add value to the work. During my time in the director's office, the November election meant a new president was coming to town (George H.W. Bush), and he would designate a new NPS director. Bill Mott retired again and James Ridenour, former state parks director from Indiana was appointed to replace him. In the transition period, the director's office and staff, including me, worked to provide briefing materials to the incoming team and to answer their many questions.

- - - - - -

In addition to the national headquarters for the National Park Service, one of ten bureaus of the Department of the Interior, the NPS has a huge presence in Washington. The NPS manages many of the monuments on the National Mall (such as the Washington Monument, Lincoln Memorial, Jefferson Memorial and the Mall itself) and numerous small park areas throughout the city. In addition, the NPS is responsible for maintaining the White House grounds and assisting with White House tours.

Because of this role at the White House, Director James Ridenour was invited for a special tour through the White House and grounds, and I was invited to go along. We both had to provide our birth dates and social security numbers ahead of time so the Secret Service could do background checks before we arrived at the White House. On a typical Friday afternoon, the president would leave for Camp David at 3:30 by helicopter from the White House grounds. Once the president left, special projects and any repairs could begin without disruption to official events. This was also time for our insiders' tour. We were escorted by the head usher, the person in charge of the executive residence and White House grounds.

I remember several interesting things about that special tour, which included the upstairs living quarters, the Lincoln Bedroom, the Truman Balcony, and the lower floor with the White House Mess (staff cafeteria). As we walked through the East Room, workers were busy replacing the windows with bullet-proof glass. The replacement windows were extremely heavy and had to be lifted into place with a small front-end loader. This piece of equipment had been brought inside in pieces and reassembled to operate on three inches of plywood temporarily placed to protect the historic floors. Work on major projects does not begin until the president leaves for Camp David or another trip, and work is halted before the president returns. All evidence of the work project vanishes with the workers. Everyone working in the White House for even a few hours must pass rigorous security checks.

I learned that the NPS contracts and pays for one exterior wall of the White House to be painted each year. This year was to be the south side, and when we were taken out on the Truman Balcony, the original stonework was scraped bare of paint in preparation for the new coating. We could plainly see scorch and burn marks on the stone – evidence of when British troops set fire to the White House in 1814 during the War of 1812. The blackened area certainly dramatized the important history contained in the White House, officially called The People's House.

The third remarkable part of the tour began when we were taken outside to a plain white van and driven into the suburbs to an unmarked warehouse-sized concrete building. As our van approached a garage door, it opened to expose another garage door on the other end of the small drive-through space. Our credentials were checked by a guard, then the other door opened, and we drove in. Once inside, it looked like a furniture warehouse. Numerous pieces of furniture were in separate floor-to-ceiling bins. Each piece had a tag that listed its history. This furniture in the White House historic collection had the tags listing past uses of each piece. For example, a chair tag might show earlier use in the study of President Jefferson and in the Blue Room by President Ford and so on. The NPS has an important role with oversight of the White House historical collections. After this interesting tour, we were driven back to the

Department of Interior and I took the Metro to our rental house in Virginia. That was quite a day, and it stood out among the many memorable experiences in our nation's capital.

The National Park Service maintains the White House grounds and historic collections. NPS also assists with public tours.

— — — — — —

Having never been to Washington for an inauguration, we were looking forward to attending some of the public activities associated with George Bush's inauguration in January 1989. We attended a special evening event at the Lincoln Memorial on the Thursday evening before the big event on Saturday. Our family arrived at the Lincoln Memorial about an hour early and ended up in good seats that were reserved but empty as the program was set to begin. Organizers don't like to have empty seats shown in news coverage, so we were encouraged to fill in. After the speech by President-elect Bush, the Beach Boys sang their popular songs for an hour. We had told our kids about the popularity of the Beach Boys, and they were eager to see them perform. When they first came out on stage, our nine-year-old daughter said in a loud voice, "What's the big deal? They are so OLD!" causing a ripple of laughter from the crowd around us. The entertainment was followed by a deafening military flyover and a spectacular fireworks presentation choreographed to patriotic music. It was an extraordinary evening, and we felt like we were a small part of history in the making.

On Inauguration Day, January 20, we rode the Metro into Washington for the grand parade down Pennsylvania Avenue. The parade had units representing all fifty states and passed the elegant viewing stand that had been constructed for the occasion in front of the White House. We read where the U.S. Postal Service removed all of the deposit boxes along Pennsylvania Avenue to prevent them from being used as a place to hide bombs, and we also heard that the manhole covers along the route were welded shut for similar reasons. After the parade, we walked to the nearest Metro along with thousands of others. We wanted to head to the Virginia suburbs, as did most of the others who crammed into the station, taking every available space. Each Orange Line train headed our way was already jammed packed, and few additional people could get on. Getting nowhere, we decided to get on the next train going in the opposite direction and get off a few stops later, only to get on the next train heading back the other way to Virginia. This lucky decision allowed us to get seats before the huge crowd pushed on at the coming stops.

– – – – – –

For the second six-month training period, I became a staff intern for the National Parks Subcommittee of the House Interior Committee. Each committee and subcommittee had a majority and a minority staff. During this time period, the Republicans in the House were in the minority, and therefore, committee staffs were smaller in number. I chose to volunteer to work for the minority staff figuring that since they had fewer staff positions, they might give me more meaningful work. I also thought I could gain valuable insights into the politics of congressional committee operations. I wrote briefing materials, suggested questions for hearings, and attended legislative hearings, mark-ups, and even floor votes. Given my work experience in national parks, I had valuable knowledge that helped the committee to better understand certain issues.

It was fascinating and a great learning experience. My staff ID also allowed me to get to places in the Capitol that were closed to the public.

– – – – – –

In Washington, the NPS had offices in two different buildings about a mile and a half apart. For fresh air and exercise, I would often walk between them, although the high humidity in summer usually meant I would arrive soaked from perspiration. Especially in the cooler evenings, I liked to walk around the National Mall, the Lincoln Memorial, the Washington Monument, and the White House. One evening I finished a long walk on the National Mall and was heading back to the Metro stop just beyond the White House. It was prior to 9/11 and security was less strict than it is today, but still the White House in particular was well guarded by the Secret Service. There were obvious silent alarm systems that paralleled the fence lines and conspicuous armed guards at each gate and on the roof of the White House.

It was getting dark and I was walking at an angle across the street toward the rounded sidewalk and the high steel fence behind the White House. The only other person I could see was a woman walking ahead of me on that rounded sidewalk. She glanced over her other shoulder, away from me, and there was no one behind her. Because of my angle of approach, I was not within her view. When I was maybe twenty feet away, she suddenly stopped and put her head close to the steel fence and quietly spoke, calling for Roy. She called his name two or three times, and out from the bushes came a heavily armed man in camouflage clothing and dark makeup on his face. He was obviously part of the White House security team, and as he came out of the bushes, he instantly saw me at the same time he saw his wife (I assume). He angrily said, "I told you not to do that!" I kept walking and did not hear more of their exchange, but it was apparent that he was unhappy about being exposed to a random stranger (me). It must be a tremendous challenge for the many Secret Service agents who spend hours on duty, often waiting or observing, needing to remain alert to various possible but unlikely threats.

– – – – – –

Meanwhile, the family visited every free museum in Washington. Our neighbors thought we were a bit nuts – always doing some "tourist thing." But of course, they could do any of those things at any time so normal procrastination meant they mostly never did. At the end of the year, when we moved to the West again, our kids said if they "never go to another museum, it would be too soon." In reality, the whole family benefited from that year in our nation's capital. The kids saw the important elements of our government, such as the Congress, the Supreme Court, the White House, and many of the departments of the Executive Branch. We enjoyed the numerous free activities and museums, and we witnessed history in the making at inaugural activities for President Bush. Toward the end of my year's program, we were all ready to get back to reality in what we hoped would be a new assignment in rural America in one of our great national parks.

The irony is that the next school year our son, Chris, who was then in seventh grade came home and excitedly announced, "Guess where the eighth-grade trip is going." We said, "Where?" to which he replied, "Washington, D.C.!" We said, "You don't want to go there, do you, since you have already been to all those places?" "Heck yes!" was his immediate reply.

– – – – – –

Superintendents from across the country occasionally got together at training sessions or the less frequent (every five to ten years) national conferences where we could learn about the latest policy directives and discuss mutual challenges. These opportunities were valuable for many reasons. The best outcome from these gatherings was the important two-way exchange of information. We would hear from the subject matter experts on proposed changes in specific programs or policies, and in turn, they would hear the field perspective from the park superintendents. Feedback from the parks was essential to make national or regional changes more effective or at least less onerous.

Evenings were generally free, and groups of us would go out for dinner or have a few drinks to talk informally. These after-hours discussions were often more worthwhile than some of the formal sessions during the day. Networking was valuable and we learned a lot from each other. We got to know our colleagues within our region or nationally. These friendships paid off when we wanted to consult someone about a difficult issue, learn more about how another superintendent handled a similar situation, or ask for a reference on a job applicant. The superintendent ranks were small in number so for better or worse, everyone had a reputation among their peers. A good reputation led to career advancement. In addition, superintendents tended to periodically move to new assignments by applying for promotions through our internal personnel system. By moving around or hiring employees from other parks, we often spent time catching up on news related to mutual friends and colleagues. Much of this talk centered on who was vying for key jobs and who was rumored to have the inside track. The common jargon for a job that was rumored to be pre-determined was "wired". Many of the rumors turned out to be wrong.

Nationwide superintendents' conferences were held at large capacity national park lodges or conference hotels, but with nearly 500 participants, which included Washington and regional office staff, adequate conference facilities were a necessity. Only four national superintendents' conferences were held during my thirty-eight-year career (Yellowstone, Saint Louis, Snowbird in Utah, and Grand Teton). These conferences usually had a few nationally known speakers and they were a great opportunity to see old friends and make new ones. As the conferences ended, I would return to my park with a box full of handouts and notes with good intentions, but the reality was that my awaiting workload took precedence, and many of these reference materials ended up on a shelf to gather dust.

At these infrequent gatherings of park superintendents, the newer superintendents often hung out together and traded stories. One of my friends, the superintendent at Homestead National Historic Site, told of the time early in his career when he was the newest ranger on the staff at Blue Ridge Parkway. As such, he was usually on call in the evening. He would remain in uniform to be available for emergencies or other call-outs. One evening the park dispatch center called to say he needed to go to the campground and take a report from two nuns who had hit and killed a bear near mile marker 138 on the parkway. When Ranger Randy got to the campground, the nuns were waiting and obviously upset. Randy tried to set them at ease, and he asked them to tell him what had happened. They said they were driving down the parkway when a bear ran in front of them just before mile marker 138, and they couldn't avoid hitting him. They were terribly upset about killing this animal. Randy asked if the bear ended up in the ditch or ran off since he had just come by that marker and he didn't see the bear along the road. They said, "Oh no, it is in the trunk." Evidently, they thought they had to bring the body in to file a report. I always laugh when I think of these two nuns in their habits heaving even a small bear into their car's trunk. It must have been adrenalin at work. Randy asked for the trunk key saying he would take care of the body. As he opened the trunk, the bear came flying out and ran into the woods. He speculated that the bear had only been only knocked unconscious when the nuns had picked it up and loaded it into the trunk. Maybe they thought there had been some other higher power that brought the bear back to life. In any case, it is a story that neither the nuns nor Randy would ever forget.

Another friend told the story of one of his rangers at Great Smoky Mountain who gave a detailed account of a situation he had encountered the previous week. He was on routine patrol and drove through one of the parking areas with an obvious sign that said: closed at dusk. Since it was now fully dark and there was a vehicle parked at the far end of the lot, Ranger Charlie who always displayed good judgment decided to check it out. There was no one in the vehicle so he shined his flashlight on nearby open areas looking for the occupants of the vehicle. He soon came upon a naked man and women making love just off the parking lot in the weeds. In his highly professional demeanor, he told them they had done three things wrong: First, they were parked in an area that was closed at dusk, and they could be cited for being in a closed area. Second, he could cite them for indecent exposure. However, he said he was not going to do either because their third mistake was lying in poison ivy. He felt the natural outcome would be punishment enough.

As colleagues took turns telling their favorite stories, a friend from Grand Teton National Park in Wyoming told of a recent call for help from two college students. Back when cell phones had just become popular, park dispatch received a call from a person high up on Middle Teton Mountain. He and his partner were stuck on a cliff and wanted to be rescued. The dispatcher followed protocol and asked a series of questions to determine how serious the situation was. Was anyone injured? No. Was anyone on medication? No. Did they have extra food and water? No. Did they have extra clothes for warmth? No. Finally, the dispatcher said to the man, "I have to ask you guys, what are you doing up there with none of the things you should have?" The caller's answer was surprising even to someone who was used to hearing all manner of excuses. The caller said, "We had all of that stuff on our floor at the apartment this morning and decided it was too much to carry, so we thought we would bring our cellphone, and if we needed something we would just call." Given that it was late in the day and there was no obvious emergency, park dispatch told the climbers that they would need to "wait until morning, and if they still needed help to call back." There was no justification for sending a search and rescue team out in the approaching darkness given that it was not an urgent matter. It was hoped that spending the night on that chilly mountainside might have been a valuable lesson.

Once at a training session in San Diego, a small group of us decided to go see the historic Hotel del Coronado, which was not only famous, but it was a magnificent building listed on the National Register of Historic Places. As we were walking through the lovely ornate hotel, there was a noisy event with big lighted ice sculptures in the main ballroom and a large crowd gathered around multiple bars and food tables. The placard at the door said, "Oscar Mayer Corporate Event." As we stood in the doorway looking in, someone approached us and asked who we were with. One of our group, a joker type, said in jest, "We are with the National PORK Service." The man said, "Oh, come on in! Have a drink and something to eat." We tried to beg off, but he insisted. Fortunately, we weren't introduced or asked to speak! However, we did enjoy the hospitality. Instead of a "joker," I should have called our funny friend a real "hot dog," which would have been most appropriate at the Oscar Mayer event.

Speaking of Oscar Mayer, the corporation has a large vehicle made to look like a giant hot dog. The vehicle is driven around the country to large events for advertising purposes. Probably 25 feet long, it looks like a hot dog in a bun and says Oscar Mayer in large letters on the side. When the hot dog vehicle showed up at Acadia one day, our rangers had to turn them away since commercial vehicles are prohibited inside the national park.

Rangers never know what to expect each day. Since commercial vehicles are not permitted in the national parks, this Oscar Mayer marketing vehicle had to have the picnic elsewhere.

- - - - - -

As my one year in Washington neared an end, I was getting anxious about where my next assignment would be. It was my responsibility to apply to job vacancies that interested me. What made this particularly stressful was that I only had a few months to find a new position. That meant I had to choose from openings available at the time. As is always the case, there would be some available positions I had no interest in because of location, quality of schools, or other circumstances that ruled them out. Family needs always played a large role in such decisions. All NPS managers had their own personal list of "dream parks" where they hoped to go someday, and I was no exception. Barb and I would spend many evenings discussing superintendent vacancies and rumors of possible openings in various parks across the country. Whenever we visited other national parks, we would look at the park facilities and challenges as well as the nearby community in case the superintendent's position would become available.

I was offered a superintendent's position in Texas, but it wasn't a place I really wanted to be, and besides, I didn't think it was a good family fit either. I applied for a few superintendent vacancies including the deputy position at Rocky Mountain National Park, one of my "dream parks." I learned I was one of forty-five qualified applicants for the job which was typical for positions in the most popular parks. I was thrilled to receive an interview, which indicated I probably was among the top three candidates. Finally, the call came from Superintendent Jim Thompson offering me the job. I didn't need to clear it with Barb or the kids; I immediately accepted. We had thirty days to make the move and we all were excited.

CHAPTER FIVE

ROCKY MOUNTAIN NATIONAL PARK, COLORADO

Deputy Superintendent, 1989-1996

The caller was planning his summer trip to Rocky Mountain National Park located near Estes Park, Colorado, and he wanted to know "where in the park can I go to see mountains?" The obvious answer (at least to park staff) was "anywhere in the park" since the national park encompasses more than sixty mountain peaks over 12,000 feet high. The national park ranges in elevation from 8,000 feet to the highest mountain in the park, Longs Peak at 14,259 feet. The park includes many great features: lush mountain valleys with abundant wildflowers and wildlife, thickly forested mountainsides below tree line, weather ravaged high peaks, cascading streams and waterfalls, and serene high mountain lakes.

The park's backcountry office kept a running list of visitors' amusing questions. A flatlander asked, "How do you climb a mountain, and what is there to do once you get on top?" A first-time backpacker asked, "Are there electrical outlets at the backcountry campsites?" Another camper asked, "Will bears like my perfume?" With a silent chuckle, friendly park staff would answer these and other questions for the many adventuresome visitors planning their trips into Rocky's extraordinary wilderness.

There are over 359 miles of trails to backpack, hike and ride on horseback. In the winter there are plenty of opportunities to snowshoe and cross-country ski. The closest towns are Estes Park on the east side and Grand Lake on the west side of the Continental Divide where accommodations, restaurants and other services are found.

Trail Ridge Road, connecting Grand Lake and Estes Park, is usually open from Memorial Day to late autumn. It is the highest continuously paved road in the United States, topping out at 12,183 feet. It allows enthusiastic visitors to see mountain peaks, high elevation lakes and open meadows often teeming with elk and other wild animals. Wildlife viewing is a major reason people come to Rocky and with good reason. In addition to large herds of elk, people enjoy seeing the moose, bighorn sheep, black bears, mule deer, eagles, hawks and scores of smaller animals that make this park their home.

Twelve miles of Trail Ridge Road are above tree line
with the high point being over 12,000 feet.

Forest Canyon Overlook on Trail Ridge Road.

With a loud crack, the ice gave way and in an instant, I was standing on the bottom of the Colorado River with snowshoes on my feet and a twenty-five-pound pack on my back. It was midwinter in Rocky Mountain National Park, and accidentally going into the river could be life threatening. I was participating in the annual river otter survey where volunteers and park staff, working in pairs, would survey the twenty miles of the Colorado River inside the park looking for signs of the playful creature. The deep snows along the river allowed observers to see otter slides and other signs that the river otters were active. The waist deep water was icy cold, and if the river current had been stronger or the water deeper, I would have been swept downstream and trapped under the ice. Other than my partner, help was miles away. The fast thinking Colorado Division of Wildlife officer extended a broken branch from the safety of the bank, and with a struggle I was able to get out of the hole and onto the bank in deep snow. Thanks to a park radio we carried, we called park dispatch for an emergency pick-up. Wet and shivering in the morning chill with air temperatures around twenty degrees, I was afraid my wet clothes would freeze stiff. I was soon picked up by a ranger on a snowmobile and heading for a hot shower and dry clothes. Later that year, the staff presented me with the first ever "Above and Below" Award for going above and beyond in my search for otter sign.

The annual counts provided important information about the number and extent of the river otter in the park since they were reintroduced several years before I came to Rocky. We particularly liked to find the otter slide marks where they play by sliding down banks onto ice or into the river. These field surveys looked for any evidence of otter activity, such as slides, runs, and tracks, and latrine sites because seeing the animals is uncommon. Trends in these annual observations indicated the population was likely stable or slowly growing in number, which meant our restoration efforts were succeeding.

Wildlife management in Rocky Mountain was an important part of our work and that meant conducting research to learn more about the various species in the park. One of the three park scientists, Hank McCutchen, was working on a multiyear study focused on the black bear population. It included having radio collars on ten to twelve bears, which could then be routinely tracked by radio telemetry. The collars worked well, thanks to batteries that needed to be replaced every two years – while the bears were in hibernation. The standard procedure was to hike and snowshoe to a den using the radio signals as his guide, tranquilize the bear using a spring-loaded syringe on the end of a jab stick, and pulling the bear from the den to collect research data on their health and reproduction. Hank would take a blood sample and make notes on other observations. He would then install a new battery in the collar before placing the bear back in the den and heading home.

As the deputy superintendent in charge of park operations, I often tagged along on various field trips, backcountry patrols, and even complex search and rescues. One fall, I asked Hank, one of our most experienced scientists, to accompany him on at least one of his winter trips to the bear dens. It turned out to be three arduous day trips up into the wintry mountains in search of black bears. I recall each of those trips to be an exhilarating and rewarding adventure even when we didn't find a bear.

My first den trip was high above Finch Lake in an area of large rockfall. We drove as close to the area as possible, then hiked a couple of miles before putting on snowshoes for the final climb up to the den site. We each carried a snow shovel to dig through deep snow looking for the den opening. After several hours, we found the den, but the bear was somewhere under a jumble of huge granite boulders on the mountainside. Normally, Hank would be lowered into the den to locate and prepare the bear to be hauled out (after being tranquilized, of course). On this day, the bear apparently sensed there was a threat and moved deep into the rocky cave, making it impossible to reach. Showing a little frustration, Hank made the decision to give up on this mission and head back before nightfall, which came early in winter.

Photo on previous page: Radio telemetry guides researchers to an approximate den location but the actual den is not always found. Photo this page: Failing to find the bear, we took the "short cut" sliding down the frozen cascades of Thousand Falls.

My second trip with Hank was particularly grueling because we snowshoed several miles up to a ridge and down into the valley where we thought the bear was, only to lose the signal, which meant we were in the wrong area altogether. Hank explained that the signal often bounced off the granite rocks and making it difficult to interpret and find the right location. So, it was back up to the ridge, and in order to beat darkness, we snowshoed toward his recommended short-cut. It turned out to be shorter in distance, but not shorter in the time required to make the steep descent toward our car. The route took us down what was called Thousand Falls, a steep frozen cascade that dropped in stages over 1,100 feet to the valley below. We would slide down the ice-covered steeper parts and then, still in snowshoes, climb over downed trees and other obstacles to get to the next slide. So, climb over or go around, slide down, climb over and around, slide, repeat. Hours later we got back to our car, and I went home wet from perspiration, cold, and exhausted.

After two arduous trips with no actual bear sightings, I was less enthusiastic about a third trip but determined to see a bear. It was planned for late March, and that meant it would not be as cold, snow would likely be more compacted, and daylight longer. We drove to the southern park boundary, and then hiked a few miles through the forest to a rocky slope with patches of snow and ice and a few small cave openings. We did not have to dig through snow to find the bear's den since it was familiar to Hank and obvious as we approached. The first step in the procedure was for Hank to be lowered into the den by his ankles with a flashlight in his mouth to determine if the bear was within reach, and if there were one or more cubs. The adult bear would be tranquilized, but it was too risky to tranquilize cubs. Upon observing a mother bear and two cubs, Hank signaled (by shaking his leg) that we were to pull him out, which we did. His assistant then prepared a spring-loaded syringe with the tranquilizer at the end of a six-foot jab stick, which looked a lot like a broom handle. Step two was for Hank to be lowered back into the den, again by his ankles, with flashlight and jab stick in one hand. He kept the other hand free to push off the rocks as he got closer to the bear. Once close enough, he would inject the mother and we would then wait fifteen minutes for the drug to take effect. We were instructed to place our packs in the den opening to block light from getting in because that might wake the hibernating bear. Hank explained that the mother bear would sense our human presence and the potential threat to her cubs. Furthermore, she would try to come out of her hibernation sleep to respond; hence the importance of the drug.

While we waited for the drug to take effect, Hank told us that once the mother was safely tranquilized, he would go back in and hand out the two cubs to be held inside our coats for warmth, a role for which I quickly volunteered. When the time was up, we lowered Hank with a harness and rope that he would place around the adult bear and use to pull her out of the den to take the required measurements and samples. The results would be recorded as part of the multiyear bear study. Just as Hank was moving to put the harness on the bear, his assistant yelled, "Quick, get him out of there." The assistant quickly explained that the syringe had not gone off, and therefore, the mother bear was likely waking up to defend her den and cubs. He said that was the first time the spring-loaded syringe had failed. On this particular day, we had taken a Denver Post reporter and photographer along, so I had sudden visions of a newspaper article with the headline of "Park researcher mauled in den by mother bear." We hurriedly pulled Hank out and explained the problem. We had to do the tranquilizer step over again using the jab stick, and this time the drug was injected properly. Once it was safe, Hank returned into the den to hand out the cubs and rope up the mother who weighed about 150 pounds, below average. Relieved that we had realized the problem before a possible nasty confrontation, we successfully completed the rest of the work.

Once the den is located, one researcher enters the den to determine if there are cubs.

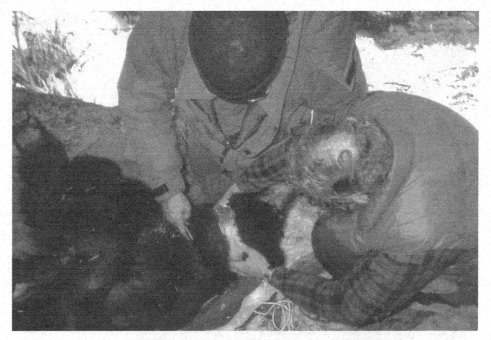

Once the adult bear is tranquilized, researchers record observations and install new collar battery before placing the bear back in the den.

The cubs were about the size of a basketball but already with big feet and claws, surprisingly about the size of my hands. One assistant was handed the female cub, which he stuffed inside his coat to keep her warm. She went right to sleep. Hank's assistant then handed me the male cub, which I tried to put inside my coat, but he was having none of it and tried to claw his way up and out.

Meanwhile, our team of five researchers and volunteers weighed the three bears, took blood samples from the mother, checked teeth, and took various measurements. Hank explained that the research was showing that the bears inside the national park were "living on the edge," so to speak. They had larger than normal territories (movements tracked by the radio collars), and they were smaller than normal black bears, which seemed to indicate that food was not as available without moving over greater distances. Mothers were averaging one cub rather than the usual two, and the cubs tended to stay with the mother longer than normal. Unlike the American grizzly bear, the black bear, which can also be brown in color, is less threatening to humans. Records indicated that human injuries or deaths from black bears were rare. However, a mother black bear will aggressively attack and fight to protect cubs – one fact that added a little extra nervousness to this den trip with the misfire of the syringe.

Once the work was done and data collected, we lowered the mother back into the den and placed the cubs on the mother's belly. The cubs are born and begin nursing while the mother is hibernating, which seems like a nice arrangement. We then covered the opening of the den with some snow and brush to try to minimize light getting into the den and reduce our scent left behind. As we hiked out, Hank told us that the mother bear will often sense the intrusion and move the cubs to a new den within a day or two. All that remained for that day was the long hike back to the cars left along the highway and a late dinner to be followed by a good night's sleep.

The next morning, my neck was both red and sore where the male cub had scratched me. Even after another day, the scratches and rash were no better, so I went to my local doctor who didn't seem to know what ointment would be best to treat a rash caused by a bear. In fact, he seemed a little skeptical of my bear story. He excused himself and returned in a few minutes. As it turned out he had called the local veterinarian for some advice, and the recommended salve cleared up the rash in a week or so.

Data collected from the 1985-1991 study indicated that Rocky Mountain National Park's population of black bears was only around twenty, and the population had one of the lowest densities and reproductive rates ever recorded. The scientists attributed this to the park's large percentage of tundra and high alpine forests, which provide little of the nutritional foods like berries that bears prefer. Bears are omnivores that eat both plants and animals. In Rocky, they eat mostly roots, berries, nuts and insects. However, there was a trend developing where bears were finding human food in garbage cans, dumpsters, and campsites in and around the park. Park managers began implementation of a bear management plan that included reducing access to human foods primarily through better trash management and efforts to educate staff and visitors about ways to reduce bear-human interactions.

The report went on to say: "Females with cubs do not breed again until the cubs have separated. Females give birth to litter sizes of one or more cubs every other year. Cubs are born in the mother's winter den with eyes closed after a two- to three-month gestation period. They continue to nurse through the first summer and often stay with the mother for up to eighteen months." The 1985-91 study found only about 40 percent of cubs in the park survived. A more recent study confirmed the total number of bears to be in the twenty to twenty-four range, but it found the cub survival rate had increased to nearly 70 percent. However, there was no explanation for the increase.

Resource managers need information on habitat use and food preferences to analyze land management decisions and their potential impact on black bear populations. For instance, black bears can be attracted to campgrounds, where food is often readily available due to camper carelessness. Habitat assessments can help identify suitable areas for relocation of problem bears that are farthest from developed campgrounds. Managers need to know the location and availability of potential denning areas so that habitat improvements might be undertaken if a lack of adequate sites exists, and to manage park lands to keep human disturbance away from potential den sites.

－ － － － － － －

Netting an elk from a moving helicopter was not easy, but the team from New Zealand worked well together and anticipated each other's needs. The pilot of the small Hughes 500 flew low and could make fast turns as needed to separate one elk from the herd. Flying over the herd got the animals moving, and soon they would divide up until one veered off on its own. Then, pursuing the lone elk as the target, the gunner would fire a net from a shotgun as he was seated in the open door of the helicopter with his feet on the skid. He was strapped in to allow him to safely lean out for the best shot. Once the net covered an elk, the animal would stop running and fall to the ground. The copter would land quickly, and the crew would rush to the elk, blindfold it to reduce stress, and install a radio collar on the neck of the animal so it could be tracked for research purposes. Within a couple of minutes, the elk was released unharmed. It was all done so quickly; no tranquilizer was needed.

This was the beginning of a new study to determine the number and distribution of the elk in Rocky Mountain and how far they would travel to winter range when the snow was too deep to feed in the park's open meadows. In addition to learning more about the range of elk, the radio collars helped researchers find the herds so numbers could be estimated from aerial photos taken periodically throughout the year. Before the formal study was initiated, we knew the numbers were growing from regular observations, but little else. Researchers were surprised to learn that after one particularly heavy snowstorm, three of the collared elk traveled from the park to Loveland, a distance of more than thirty miles. Two of the three never came back. It may be that the increasing numbers of elk were forcing some to find new habitat to occupy. Using the study data, the park developed its first elk management plan to provide park managers better information and criteria for making decisions.

Photo on previous page: Using a small helicopter to net elk for research purposes.
Photo this page: Collar number 56 is quickly placed and the elk is released.

- - - - - -

My wife, Barb, and I, along with our son and daughter (now ten and eight), went into the park on many September evenings to watch the big bull elk gather their harems as part of mating season called the rut. During the mating season, the handsome, mature bull elk compete with one another for the right to breed with a herd of females. Prime bulls, eight to nine years old, stand the best chance of mating.

Visitors were especially thrilled to hear the bulls bugle, which is a high pitched almost squeal with a series of grunts at the end. During rutting season, elk gather in the large open meadow areas. The younger males, called spike bulls because they have single antlers on each side of the head, are usually off in a group by themselves since they are not mature enough to take part. The majestic bulls with huge racks prance around with their heads held high bugling, hoping to attract more females. Within the gathering herds, the larger antlered males, now weighing as much as 1,000 pounds, move nervously among the bands of smaller females. Sometimes one or more females will try to move from one harem to another, which might lead to a confrontation between bulls. They strut and fake charge, but occasionally they may lock horns and twist and turn until one bull breaks away. I remember a rare instance where a large bull elk was killed by another when an antler pierced his skull.

Wildlife viewing is a major visitor attraction.

Visitors stopping to photograph wildlife produce "animal jams".

On a typical fall afternoon and early evening, hundreds of visitors line the roads along the meadows to observe. Many bring food and beverage to enjoy while they watch – almost like tailgate parties at a college football game. The park recruited and trained a large group of volunteers to be part of what we called the Elk Bugle Corp to help keep visitors back a safe distance, direct traffic, and provide explanations for the animal behaviors. Moraine Park, Horseshoe Park, Upper Beaver Meadows, and the Kawuneeche Valley were the largest meadows with the heaviest elk concentrations in the fall. The term "park" in the name of a location, such as Estes Park or Moraine Park, is defined as an open area surrounded by mountains.

Rangers on horseback often visit the most popular meadows to assist with crowd control. One evening, I rode along on Smokey, the horse Ranger Jim Schlinkman had ready for me at the nearby parking lot where we met. I had ridden Smokey before, but this time he seemed nervous and stressed. He would rear his head back and neigh more than usual. I thought maybe it was my horsemanship (or lack thereof), but when we arrived at Horseshoe Park, we encountered Ranger Denise who took one look at Smokey and said, "Do you know that his bit is upside down?" No wonder Smokey was acting uncomfortable with the more pointed side of the bit hitting the roof of his mouth. After the equipment adjustment, Smokey was fine, and I was relieved.

Elk are one of the largest members of the deer family. Large males, called bulls, average 600-800 pounds compared to the females, called cows, which weigh between 400-500 pounds. Adult males stand four and a half to five feet at the shoulder. The elk population in the national park was estimated to number about 1,000 grouped in various herds, with as many as several hundred individuals in one herd. Prior to mating season, the mature bull elk would often stay in separate groups as did the immature spike bulls. The females along with their calves would normally graze together in groups. Dark brown manes, light-brown bodies and white rumps characterize both sexes. They grow a thicker coat of hair each winter which they shed each spring. Losing their winter coat in clumps makes them look pretty "ratty," but soon the elk grow their fresh, shiny summer coat.

Only males have antlers, which grow up to an inch a day in the spring and then fall off each winter. The antlers grow with a protective layer of velvety skin that the bulls scrape off by rubbing their antlers on tree trunks once the antlers are fully grown. A full set of antlers can weigh forty pounds or more. Elk have a large range and move as their food availability changes over the seasons. In the summer, some herds feed on tundra vegetation at higher elevations, while others stay in the lower meadows in and around the park. In winter, they move to lower elevations of the park and surrounding community, and some go much farther to the Front Range (Fort Collins and Loveland) to avoid deep snows. In early summer, we would often see groups of females and calves grazing together in our Estes Park neighborhood while the bulls were off in separate groups.

Calving usually happens in tall grassy or brush areas away from the herd. Elk calves are born from late May into June and weigh about 30 pounds. While hiking one morning, I was fortunate to see a wobbly newborn calf still steaming in the cold mountain air. Most cows give birth to one calf, but they sometimes have two. Newborns have spots, which fade away by late summer. Calves can join the herd after two weeks and are weaned at two months old. They also make sounds that remind me of a short high-pitched bark when looking for their mother. The cows bark to warn of danger, and the calves make a sound called a mew to keep track of one another. Cows are extremely protective of their calves, so visitors are told to use caution around elk at this time of year.

- - - - - -

One particularly interesting bird is the peregrine falcon that historically nested in Rocky Mountain National Park, but due to the pesticide DDT, the population was in serious decline throughout the United States in the 1950s, '60s and '70s. In 1978, the peregrine falcon was placed on the endangered species list, and a restoration program was initiated in Rocky Mountain National Park in cooperation with the Colorado Division of Wildlife.

Wildlife biologist bands peregrine chicks and then returns them to hack box below.

The peregrine falcon is a bird of prey (raptor) and the fastest animal alive. The bird feeds almost exclusively on other medium-sized birds such as pigeons, doves, and songbirds taken in midair. The peregrine does this in a high-speed dive that has been documented at over 200 miles an hour.

Pairs of peregrines mate for life, and they return to the same nest every year. The birds usually lay their eggs on a high mountain ledge in a shallow hollow scraped in loose soil or gravel with no other nesting material added. The courtship flight includes a mix of aerial acrobatics, precise spirals, and steep dives. The male passes prey it has caught to the female in midair. To make this possible, the female actually flies upside-down to receive the food from the male's talons.

Golfers often have to play around elk on the Estes Park golf course.

Peregrine falcon recovery teams bred the species in captivity. The chicks were then placed in hack boxes installed on an appropriate high mountain ledge to encourage the birds to return there as adults. The chicks were usually fed through a chute or with a hand puppet that looked like a peregrine's head, so they do not become accustomed to or imprint on humans. When they are old enough, the hack box is opened, allowing the bird to begin to move its wings. As the fledgling gets stronger, feeding is reduced, forcing the bird to learn to hunt. Once the chicks learn to fly and leave the nest, we say it has fledged.

One summer I accompanied the park biologist to the hack box on Deer Mountain. We took the easier hiking route to the top of the mountain, and he was then lowered to the nest site by rope. He returned with two chicks to be banded and then placed back in the nest in the box on the side of the mountain. One of the parent falcons was overhead hovering and diving at us, attempting to ward off the perceived threat. We retreated as soon as we completed the task, but the banding program provided excellent population information. The successful hacking program at Rocky stopped in 1991. Because of the great success of hacking projects at Rocky and many other places nationwide, the peregrine falcon was taken off the threatened and endangered species list in 1999.

– – – – – –

I loved the first year of each of my new park assignments, and arriving at Rocky Mountain National Park as the new deputy superintendent (chief of operations) was no exception. In fact, the whole family was excited about moving from Washington, D.C., where I had spent the last year in a mid-level management development program for field managers to get the Washington experience. Going from a noisy, crowded urban area to a small town on the edge of a great wilderness national park was a real thrill for the entire family. Since Rocky was one of the crown jewels, and almost every park ranger dreamed of going there at some point in their career, I was eager to begin meeting the employees and learning about the park.

One night during the first weeks in our new house on the edge of Estes Park, we awoke to a loud thumping coming from outside our bedroom. As it continued, I went to the patio door and turned on the porch light to find twelve to fifteen large elk walking across our deck. The wooden deck had no railings since it was almost flush with the ground. As it turned out, our back yard often had elk, deer or coyotes standing around or even sleeping under the trees. Yard is really a misnomer since we left our property in its natural state consisting of tall ponderosa pines, scattered granite outcrops, and pine needle duff. We enjoyed the fact that we had little yard work to do. We hung a couple of cylindrical bird feeders from the trees and found out the hard way that they had to be at least ten feet off the ground. Any lower, and the elk could stand on their hind legs, stick their tongue in the bottom hole, and drain all the sunflower seed within a few minutes.

We were excited when we twice had fawns born in our yard or just outside our split rail fence. One never knew what you would see looking out our patio door in the morning. Animals, large and small, were moving though or just hanging out. We particularly liked watching the elk grazing inside and just beyond our fence. Every year, we would see a particular male elk in and around our yard. This bull had a deformed antler on one side that turned sharply downward. When this elk wanted to graze, it had to turn its head to the side or else the deformed antler would hit the ground first, preventing the animal from eating normally. The curious thing was that while elk lose their antlers each fall, this elk had the same deformed antler return each spring. Our daughter said it was having "a bad hair day."

The elk's deformed antler grew back the same each year.

75

This handsome deer buck was often in our yard.

In addition to elk, it was not unusual to see mule deer, coyotes, bighorn sheep, fox, long-tail weasels (brown in summer, white in winter), and occasionally black bears and moose. We enjoyed seeing wildlife as we drove in and around the park, and we especially enjoyed seeing a variety of wild animals around our house. Deer, elk, and coyotes were often in our yard, even lying down for hours at a time. Once our miniature dachshund was on one side of the patio door and a yearling elk was on the other side, standing on our deck almost nose to nose with the dog. It seemed that they were both curious.

Wildlife in our back yard – mule deer fawns born there
and a small herd of elk around our house.

Coyotes were known to take cats and small dogs, like our miniature dachshund. One Saturday I was making lunch and happened to glance outside and see a large coyote slowly sneaking up on our dog, Sam. She was sitting in

77

her pen made of chicken wire where she loved to sit for hours and watch the ground squirrels and birds come and go. On this day, she was oblivious to the approaching threat that would have caused her disappearance. Coyotes attack from downwind so the prey (our dog) doesn't catch their scent. I ran outside with a broom and yelled at the coyote to leave. It stopped its advance, looked at me and then the dog a couple of times, as if it was calculating its chances. Could it get the dog and escape, or was it time to retreat? Finally, the animal decided to wait for another day and wandered off. The dog didn't know it had almost been lunch for a bunch of coyotes.

One evening in early December, we were on our way to our first park Christmas party held in Estes Park at the downtown Holiday Inn, and all traffic was stopped by a large herd of elk crossing the main street in a long line. Estes Park, particularly the meadow areas, was prime elk winter range. Elk would move from the higher elevations where snow was too deep to the lower open meadows to graze. We would often see large groups of elk in open areas of the town, including the local golf course. It was not unusual for summer golfers to play around elk, which added to the unique experience.

My wife, a registered nurse, worked for a local doctor named Tom Nichol who was an avid golfer. He would often play nine holes several times a week after the office closed. One day he told his staff that he played the evening before and had an encounter with a female elk. He hit into a group of elk with the ball rolling near one female. She picked up the ball in her mouth and started walking away with it. Deciding it was not edible, she dropped it into a sand trap. Doctor Nichol said, "You have to play it where it lies, and maybe someday an elk will drop my ball in the hole."

Just outside of town and on the edge of the national park is the YMCA of the Rockies. There are enough cabins and lodges to have a few thousand people staying there each evening. It is so extensive; it has its own zip code. Guests were thrilled to see elk roaming though the complex or just resting in the open areas. One particular great bull elk spent many hours on the YMCA grounds, returning year after year, and he became known as Samson. He had a magnificent set of antlers, and I am sure he appeared in thousands of photos taken by guests. One fall Samson was shot by a poacher on the YMCA grounds. Guests witnessed the shooting, and chased the shooter who ran from the area leaving his truck behind. His identity was quickly known, and Division of Wildlife officers cited him. Present and past guests were outraged. A website was created, and the case was closely followed by people all over the country. When the poacher appeared in court, hundreds of Samson fans turned out to demand justice. The poacher was found guilty and sentenced to prison time. It was a sad ending to magnificent Samson, but his memory and photos will live on in the hearts of many people thrilled by his presence.

— — — — — —

My wife, Barb, volunteered for what she called crossing guard duty but not at the local school. The bighorn sheep, the largest wild sheep in North America, would come down the appropriately named Bighorn Mountain and cross the main park road to get to Sheep Lakes. There were minerals in the soil in and around the lakes that the bighorn sheep needed. This mineral lick attracted sheep almost daily to Horseshoe Park. Without the help of volunteers, the steady traffic on the park's main road would prevent the bighorns from crossing. When sheep were spotted coming down the mountain, the volunteers would stop traffic in both directions and allow them to cross. Most visitors, particularly those in the front of the line, thought the inconvenience was well worth it since many of them got great photos of the sheep.

Volunteers stop traffic so bighorn sheep can cross the main park road.

– – – – – –

The most common complaint from Estes Park residents is the howling of winter winds several days a week through the winter months. We thought it was a joke when people talked about the strong winds creating waves in their toilet, but we soon learned it was true. The waves are caused by the wind blowing across the roof vent pipes. We also learned that the Safeway on the hill in town did not want people to take shopping carts into the parking lot during the winter because the strong wind slams them into parked cars. We were cautioned to park with the front of the car into the wind because parking the opposite way might cause the door to bend backward in a strong gust. I can remember sitting in my car at a traffic light or stop sign and rocking back and forth in the wind, or having dirt and small rocks blown into the windshield.

– – – – – –

One disappointment for both Chris and Kelly was the Estes Park school policy on snow days. In Washington, school could be canceled on the mere forecast of snow the next day, mostly because the metropolitan area has infrequent snowstorms, and the city did not have the equipment or experience to handle even a couple of inches of snow. On the other hand, Estes Park received plenty of snow, so the local rule was that snow had to be up to the bumpers of the school buses before classes were canceled. Our kids described this policy as terribly "unfair."

– – – – – –

Barb loves holidays and seasonal decorations. She particularly likes Halloween. Estes Park celebrated Halloween downtown where area residents gathered in costume and merchants handed out treats. The main street was closed to traffic, and ghosts and goblins roamed the streets. Barb learned that the local veterinarian held a Halloween contest. If you brought your costumed pet in on Halloween you could get a free shot for the pet. If you and your pet both came in costume, you could compete for a year's free vet service. This was right up Barb's alley. She made a body suit for our dachshund, Samantha, and glued cotton balls all over it to make her a sheep. Barb then went as Little Bo Peep – and they won. She then stayed in costume and went downtown with the dog. Samantha was not thrilled about this idea, but she liked the dog treats from merchants. That same evening the Headless Horseman and Lady Godiva (in a body suit) appeared in town. Another year Samantha went as a hot dog with a bun suit, and Barb went as a jar of mustard. In Maine our dog had a lobster costume that generated many laughs because Abbey was low to the ground. Barb continues to dress up our dog and take her around to nursing homes and schools just to bring smiles to the faces of strangers.

– – – – – –

When I arrived as Rocky's new chief of operations, I was intent on getting to know the people and the park as quickly as possible. I spent time with each of the division chiefs (departments like resource management, visitor protection, interpretation) to learn about their piece of the total park operations picture. I particularly welcomed opportunities to get out into the park with colleagues to better understand park resources and current issues while meeting more employees as we saw some of the field projects that were underway.

81

With that in mind, within my first two weeks on the job, I agreed to take a hike up to Spruce Lake with the chief scientist for the park, Dave Stevens, to meet some researchers and learn about their ongoing field research. Spruce Lake was a high mountain lake that required an uphill hike of about four miles on an established trail as far as Fern Lake, and another mile or so climbing without benefit of a marked trail. I think we gained about 2,500 feet in elevation in those five miles, which seemed dramatic and tiring given that I was not yet acclimated to Colorado elevations. Washington, D.C., was near sea level, while Rocky Mountain National Park varied from 8,000 feet to well over 14,000 feet. That meant climbing a flight of stairs could even seem like hard work. Naturally, the hike to Spruce Lake took longer than I thought it would, and I remembered along the way that I had invited the superintendent to our house for dinner at 6 p.m. After quick introductions at Spruce Lake and a short briefing, I decided to return down the mountain by myself in order to get home in time, while Dave stayed to finish his meeting. I should have known better, but I was confident of getting back to Fern Lake and the main trail without the chief scientist. After all, I did have a good topographic map and park radio in my pack.

As I bushwhacked downhill, the lightly traveled informal trail disappeared and my concern steadily grew. What if I missed the main trail? What if I was not home when my boss arrived? Of course, I could use the radio, but I could think of nothing worse than to radio headquarters and tell everyone listening that I was lost. After studying the map and observing surroundings for what seemed like the tenth time, I finally reached the main trail. With great relief, I hurried on to headquarters and then home in time to greet the superintendent with a few minutes to spare.

During those first few weeks as the new kid on the block, I focused on meeting employees, reviewing key documents such as the park's general management plan, and learning about park resources that we were charged to protect. I also got a chance to take an orientation flight around the key features, such as Longs Peak and Bear Lake. On this flight, we flew right over one of our high mountain open-air privies (side walls but no roof), and there was someone sitting on the toilet. They gave me a friendly wave so I waved back. On another occasion, I decided to take a longer lunch break and hike to the nearest back-country campsite to check it out. In uniform and with my park radio in hand, I hiked to the nearest site, which was a mile from the trailhead. Each campsite had a name, and this one was called "Over the Hill." As I walked up and over the hill, the campsite was suddenly right in front of me. Lying there on a camp pad was a topless woman with her eyes closed. I made an abrupt turn to quietly leave without disturbing her when a voice came across my radio at a most inopportune time. Startled, she looked up, and I said, "Excuse me, just checking campsites," and I quickly disappeared back over the hill.

— — — — — —

About one third of Rocky is above tree line (11,400 feet) and is considered alpine tundra where trees cannot grow. Right at tree line, the trees were stunted and usually twisted by the wind. Some people called these one-sided trees "flag trees" since all the branches grow in the direction of the wind.

Above tree line, in the tundra areas, we would often see and hear pikas, small mammals that are part of the rabbit family, even though they look more like a hamster. They have big round ears and a high-pitched whistle or peep as they warn others of our approach. They live in the loose rocks and scurry about gathering grass for the winter. A medium-sized bird called a ptarmigan also lives in the rocks on the tundra. Unless they move, you can easily miss them since they blend in with the tundra changing colors from brown in summer to white in the winter. They have a small, bright orange patch over the eye but otherwise almost perfect camouflage. They prefer to run away rather than fly.

Bighorn sheep graze on the tundra..

We often told people that on the tundra, June was spring, July was summer, August was fall, and the rest was winter. Obviously, the growing season was short and so were most of the plants. The vegetation is primarily grasses, sedges, wildflowers, and low-growing shrubs. For most alpine plant species, growth and reproduction are strongly limited by environmental conditions and thin soils. Many of the alpine wildflowers are quite beautiful, and I love their names like sky pilot, fringed gentian, alpine paintbrush, elephant head, alpine primrose, snow buttercup, and forget-me-not.

Hiking above tree line was special with expansive views, alpine wildflowers, distant peaks, and high mountain lakes, and opportunities to see elk, bighorn sheep, and pikas. A truly special time was when the clouds settled into the valleys, filling them with "cotton." If you were up on Trail Ridge Road or on the tundra, you could be higher than the clouds with blue sky above. It was spectacular, quite a treat.

Top: So called "flag trees" because strong winds force
growth to one side. The trunks are twisted too.
Bottom: Wildflowers on the tundra – above tree line (11,400')

－ － － － － －

Wildland fire is a particular threat in the arid West, which includes all of the forested areas in Colorado. Historically, because all fires were thought to be destructive, they were put out as quickly as possible. Without a natural fire regimen, montane forests, like those in Rocky, became denser and more susceptible to severe crown fires (hot, fast moving fires at the tops of the trees). The health of these forests declined. In addition, decades of fire suppression resulted in greater density of the forests, which reduced the amount of sunlight, nutrients, or water reaching the soil. Weakened trees become more susceptible to pests, such as the spruce budworm and mountain pine beetle. This became a serious problem in Rocky Mountain National Park. Almost all the lodgepole pine on the west side of the park died over a ten-year period beginning in 2000, resulting in a much greater fire risk. As a result, Timber Creek Campground on the west side is almost devoid of trees. Perhaps the name should be changed.

In general, we have learned after many decades of fire suppression that some fire is not only good for the forests, but essential in some cases (like redwood and sequoia forests). Therefore, land managers have worked to allow some naturally occurring fires to burn under certain conditions, and we have also reintroduced fire, or controlled burns, when appropriate. Rocky Mountain was one of several western parks that had a resident Hotshot fire crew (the Alpine Hotshots). Hotshots are the best of the best wildland firefighters and were among the first crews called when large fires developed anywhere in the country. Having the Hotshots on hand, in addition to other trained staff, we initiated some controlled burns or management fires to reduce fuel loads (dead and downed trees and brush) and decrease overall fire risk. These management fires would only be started after careful planning and when a strict set of preconditions were met, including an adequately trained staff and equipment at the ready.

While I was at Rocky, we had one major wildfire, called a "project fire," that required mobilization of 150 firefighters from around the West. This fire, the Mount Cairns Fire, in June 1994 occurred on the west side of the park. It burned for about three weeks and blackened some 300 acres, considered small compared to major fires in other parks. A project fire will have an incident command team in charge and an established fire camp. These camps are set up by contractors and include semi tractor-trailer kitchens, dining facilities, showers, toilets, and sleeping areas covered with tents. Firefighting in mountain terrain is hard, dirty work and you can imagine how much these men and women eat. Superintendent Homer Rouse and I went over to the camp one evening to express our support and appreciation, and we joined them for dinner. Second helpings and even thirds were not uncommon, but not to worry, obesity was not an issue due to long hours of strenuous work. Homer and I skipped the seconds but not dessert.

Crews head out to work a fire line.

Wildland firefighters eat well after long hours of hard work on the fire line.

- - - - - -

Rocky Mountain had a large horse operation to cover the park's 465 square miles of rugged terrain. The park horse program also included mules as pack animals to take tools and equipment into the backcountry for project work, often assisting various crews working in isolated areas. A couple of employees held the more unusual job classification of animal packer, and they would be responsible for loading the mules for backcountry trips. It was important to pack and distribute the weight properly or problems could arise along the way.

Rangers often patrol the backcountry either on foot or horseback. Visitors like to see rangers out in the park, especially on horses. Rangers provide helpful information, emergency medical services, search and rescue services, and initial response on wildfires. They also help protect park resources by educating park users on proper etiquette in the park and wilderness, and provide safety messages to reduce the need for emergency responses. In addition, rangers on backcountry patrol perform minor maintenance, such as removing a tree blocking the trail, repairing a trail sign, or cleaning a campsite. They clean and stock remote privies and dig new holes when the existing ones are full. They also check campers for the required backcountry permit, and this gives them an opportunity to offer a friendly hello and any area information the campers might need. When necessary, rangers enforce the rules and regulations using the lowest level of action, such as education, appropriate to the situation.

As we rode our horses up the trail, I was thinking about the tremendous experience the young people have as they work on a project deep in the park's wilderness. For youth, working and living in a national park is a summer job they will never forget. We were heading toward a remote spike camp set up just for this project some eight miles from the nearest road. A spike camp is a group of tents, food supplies, and other equipment hauled in by pack mules to establish a temporary camp for an isolated project. Hiking in that far, working for a few hours, and then hiking back out would leave little time to get the project done. A spike camp is both more efficient and a better experience for the participants.

The SCA (Student Conservation Association) crew had an experienced supervisor and a cook to provide meals and snacks for these students during their six-week wilderness trail project. They were working on a section of trail that needed improved drainage, trail surface maintenance, and a new bridge. Materials such as logs for the bridge or stone for trail base or drainage work were collected from near the worksite but off the trail far enough not to be seen by hikers. Tall, straight trees had to be cut, and the logs would have to be peeled. In addition, large rocks had to be crushed or broken up for use as trail base. Sometimes, materials such as gravel or wooden planks were flown in by helicopter or packed in by mules. Trail crews appreciated comments from visitors who often thanked the workers for their efforts.

Members of the park management team would occasionally visit these projects to see the progress and let the volunteers know we appreciated their hard work. Midway through their experience working on this isolated project, the chief of maintenance, the trails foreman, the district ranger, and I took park horses and rode out to visit the SCA project. Unbeknownst to them, we also carried with us some mail, and more importantly, ice cream on dry ice with all the possible toppings. Our surprise visit was welcomed by the crew who offered big smiles and friendly greetings. Their eyes got as big as ice cream bowls when we pulled out the mail and the ice cream. I saw one young man fill his bowl with three large scoops of ice cream and add several toppings at once before devouring the whole thing in a few minutes, only to go for seconds. We didn't need to worry about leftovers because there was nothing left except dirty bowls. The students proudly showed us their work, and most made positive comments about this summer work experience. Many young people will tell you that finishing worthy projects and living in a wilderness spike camp for the summer is a life-changing experience. As we left, I wondered if the sugar over-load would make anyone sick later that day, however, they certainly enjoyed the surprise visit.

Very happy Student Conservation Association volunteers
after a surprise visit bringing mail and ice cream.

— — — — — —

In 1914, Doctor Dillingham was leading a horse with his son in the saddle toward Fall River Pass when a lightning strike killed the doctor and the horse instantly. His nine-year-old son survived, probably because the saddle insulated him. So, when I was riding in a string of horses headed to one of the backcountry patrol cabins for the night, lightning and thunder in the distance raised my level of stress. It was already raining, and I was thinking about the metal shoes on the horses and the fact that I was a high point up there in the saddle. We had little choice but to continue, and fortunately, we arrived without incident, although pretty wet despite our rain slickers. However, riding for a couple of hours with my muscles tensed due to the storm resulted in severe back pain for the next few days. Because I wasn't riding horses regularly, my infrequent rides often produced a leg rash from the rubbing of leather and pant leg. Some experts claimed that wearing pantyhose eliminated the friction and the rash, but I could never bring myself to try it.

— — — — — —

Ranger Jim was waiting for me at the trailhead at 6 a.m. with two horses saddled and ready to go. As the chief of operations for the park, I liked to get out into the field with employees and see the park from their perspective. Today's trip was a twenty-two-mile round trip ranger patrol on horseback to Lakes Nanita and Nakoni, lightly visited because of their remoteness. We were on the trail for the entire day and saw less than five other people.

Caretti, as everyone called him, was a ranger's ranger. He was tall, lean, and handsome with his mustache and flat hat. Rangers had many skills, such as climbing, emergency medical training, wildland firefighting, and horsemanship. Caretti had brought a new horse named Beamer for me to ride that day. Beamer was donated to the park by a retiring rancher from Oklahoma who wanted his horse to spend his days in a natural setting while also performing community service work. This was Beamer's first season at Rocky, and we were still learning how well he would adapt to the routine of life in a national park.

91

The author on Smokey one of the many park horses used
for backcountry patrol and work projects.

It didn't take long for me to begin to wonder what kind of day I was in for. As we rode up the trail, we soon came to a shallow creek that we would need to cross. Caretti and his horse rode right through the shallow creek, but Beamer froze stiffly, making it plain he was not going to cross willingly. Caretti said we needed to make him cross, so he wouldn't be afraid next time. We pushed and pulled him through the water, and once across I remounted and we rode on. A few miles later, we approached a wooden bridge over a small gorge, and you guessed it, Beamer froze again. I couldn't get him to go, so Caretti said we should make him cross like we did with the creek. I am sure it was a funny scene as Caretti pulled on the reins and I pushed from the side until Beamer reluctantly crossed the bridge. It looked like it might be a longer day than I anticipated. Since our actions didn't seem to fit with that competent outdoorsman image of the park ranger, I was glad there were no witnesses.

As we neared Lake Nakoni, high in the mountains, the trail curved around a ledge and into the basin with the beautiful blue lake. However, I just knew that getting around that exposed ledge was going to be a problem for Beamer. Sure enough, it took both of us to push and pull him around, making me nervous in the process given that a fall would result in serious injuries or worse. At one point on that ledge, which had a broad rounded edge to it, Caretti's horse started to slip toward the abyss, but since he had many years of experience on his horse, he adeptly got the horse on safer ground. Had that been me, the outcome may have been more tragic.

As we sat at the edge of this deep blue lake surrounded by majestic peaks and snowfields with not another person in sight, I said to Caretti, "Jim, I have to ask two questions. Why do we have Beamer? And second, why did you pick him for me today?" His response was something to the effect that the lead wrangler thought this trip was the best opportunity to test Beamer. Also, since Caretti had ridden the same well-trained horse for many years, they thought it would be okay to let me take Beamer on a "test drive." As it turned out, that was Beamer's first and last season at Rocky.

- - - - - -

Dante was our tallest and most handsome horse, and this day he was being ridden by a County Commissioner, Jim Disney. We were on a daylong outing to familiarize local officials with some of the challenges of managing a park the size of Rocky. Like many mountain trails, this one climbed a series of tight switchbacks. Because the trail was in steep terrain, the edges of the trail were lined with logs to hold the surface material and reduce erosion. Each segment before the next switchback was relatively short. Our leader decided the horses needed a rest about midway up the switchbacks, so we stopped and sat on our horses in place. With short segments, we were kind of stacked up the mountainside with two horses on each of several levels.

Dante was the second to last horse in line, right in front of me. Suddenly there was the sound of splitting wood as Dante stepped on the log edge and it gave way. Dante and rider went crashing down the mountainside and I heard, "Whoa, Dante! Whoa!" several times as brush and tree branches gave way. I was on Smokey, and that meant I was the last in line because Smokey did not like to have another horse behind him. I mean he *really* did not like it, and if one approached, he would try to kick it with his back legs. As a somewhat reluctant horseman, I would quickly get off at any sign of trouble and hold the reins. I jumped off in case the commotion would spook Smokey or another horse. It was while I was standing there, that Smokey, perhaps accidentally, stepped on my foot. It seemed quite on purpose. Luckily, I was wearing steel-toed boots. Having gotten Dante under control, Jim brought him back up the trail with only minor scrapes. We were all relieved because it could have been much worse for both horse and rider. This was the second or third time that I wondered if getting out in the field for me should not involve the use of a horse. Walking was my preferred method of travel in the backcountry.

— — — — —

The SCA students doing the isolated trail project were part of a large VIP (Volunteers in Parks) program at Rocky Mountain and other parks across the country. Volunteers were important at every national park where I worked. In any given year Rocky Mountain had several thousand volunteers (individuals, families, organized groups). Some would volunteer for a few hours on a trail project or litter cleanup, while others would come regularly throughout the summer. I have talked to families who spend one day of their vacation volunteering to teach their children the value of giving something back.

I remember one couple from Virginia who came each summer to drive a park truck picking up litter along the roadsides. The couple enjoyed helping keep Rocky's roadsides clean. That couple once found an uncashed $4,500 check along the road and turned it in to me. When I called the bank and gave them the name on the check, they said "Oh, that guy, he is always losing things." Another retired doctor came each summer to paint picnic tables and signposts. We received many compliments from visitors about how clean and well maintained the park looked, thanks to these folks.

Volunteers would work in maintenance, administration, search and rescue, education, campground management, or visitor information roles at a visitor center or out on the trails. They wore a volunteer uniform and often worked alongside park staff. One of my favorite volunteers was Nina, who worked many days at the Wild Basin Ranger Station, and every year at Christmas she brought delicious peanut butter fudge for all to enjoy. It is safe to say that we couldn't operate the national parks at our usual high standards and adequately serve the public needs without these many dedicated volunteers. We would try to recognize and appreciate our repeat volunteers with picnics or evening events like pie night. I made it a point to learn the names of many volunteers and to visit some of them as they worked to improve the park. Expressions of appreciation were always welcomed. Projects would sometimes display a sign that said, "Volunteers at work," and park visitors would often thank the volunteers they encountered.

- - - - - -

Most weekends I spent in the park talking with employees, talking to visitors, or hiking park trails with the family. Being a goal-oriented person, I decided to make a personal goal of hiking all 350 miles of trails in the park in three years. It forced me to see every corner of the park, observe park use, and see firsthand some of the challenges of managing a park of 265,000 acres. Initially I didn't realize that I would need to hike more than 500 miles to get to some trail segments that I could not cover without repeating other segments already hiked. Of course, the family went on many of those hikes, which I think they saw as a mixed blessing.

One time, after seeing a beautiful lake from a helicopter, I enthusiastically recommended a weekend family hike to this lake. It turns out the terrain looks different from a helicopter, and getting to this beautiful lake was more difficult than I thought. We even encountered a steep cliff area that required us to add a significant detour to an already strenuous hike. After a great deal of complaining we decided to turn back, and I agreed to consult topographic maps and make sure my destinations were family friendly for future hikes. My wife still reminds me of that less than ideal experience.

One of my favorite family adventures was the hike up the Glacier Gorge, coming first to beautiful Loch Vale, which demanded a brief rest to enjoy the spectacular lake surrounded by majestic peaks. Hiking on, the trail skirts around the side of the lake teeming with native cutthroat trout before heading farther up the gorge. We were soon following a fast flowing cold and clear mountain stream uphill to Timberline Falls. The trail climbs alongside the falls, and with heavy spring runoff, water was also running over the rocks we were climbing. In addition, we were getting wet from the spray coming from the main falls just feet away. When we topped out, we were looking at the pretty Lake of Glass. When calm, it gives beautiful reflections of the high mountain cirque surrounded by McHenry's Peak, Thatchtop, Taylor Peak, and Taylor Glacier. Beyond Lake of Glass, the trail stays close to the lake and climbs to the next shelf where you arrive at Sky Pond – simply spectacular. This nine-mile round trip hike, with elevation gain of 1,700 feet, is extraordinary because every feature along the way is worth the hike by itself. In fact, this was my eleven-year-old daughter's favorite hike. I recall another day when we reached the top of Timberline Falls, we were almost blown backward and possibly off the high point by strong winds. Normally calm as the name implies, winds that day created white caps on Lake of Glass. We saw no reflections that day, but it was a good memory just the same.

Our family hike to Sky Pond climbing alongside Timberline
Falls to Lake of Glass and Sky Pond beyond.

A favorite weekend hike on the Ute Trail across the tundra,
hiking generally down from nearly 12,000'.

Another memorable day during my quest to hike every trail in the park was the one to Lion Lake, an offshoot of the Thunder Lake trail. Lion Lake #1 is 6.8 miles from the trailhead, with a gain of over 3,000 feet in elevation. On the way, you pass Copeland Falls, Calypso Cascades, Ouzel Falls, and Ouzel Lake, all beautiful spots worthy of stops. Barb and I arrived at Lion Lake #1 where we encountered a lot of wetland and boggy area that we had to find our way around. We continued up the trail another half mile past Trio Falls and on to Lion Lake #2. Our destination was Snowbank Lake appropriately named due to a large snow overhang at the upper end of the lake. These spectacular lakes are in a terraced basin framed by Pilot Mountain (12,222 feet), Mount Alice (13,310 feet), and Mount Orton (11,724 feet). We rested on a bank overlooking Snowbank Lake with its namesake at the opposite end.

Heading back toward Lion Lake #1 and down to the trailhead, another seven-plus miles, I decided to avoid the boggy end of Lion Lake #1 and cross the lake on some rocks we could see just below the surface. I started across and picked up momentum going rock to rock. My foot slipped off one rock, and stupidly my reaction was to try to run the last fifteen yards across the submerged rocks. I basically did a face plant into the bank in front of me, with my lower body in the water. In the process, I sprained my ankle. It was not only painful, but it was going to make the return hike much more difficult. My wife, a Registered Nurse, wisely advised me to keep my ankle high boot on for support as I limped down the trail. The park radio I always carried was wet and not operable, so help was a long time off if I couldn't hike out on my own. Fortunately, I made it down the trail before swelling made walking impossible. Keeping my boot on seemed to make the difference. Despite that fall, it was a truly extraordinary hike with many great features to appreciate. Once home, I put the radio in a bucket of uncooked rice for a week to dry it out and, fortunately, it was still usable for future outings in the park.

- - - - - -

On another day in the field, as we called it, I arranged for the Chief of Resources Management Craig Axtell and West Unit Manager Jock Whitworth to hike with me to Mount Ida from Trail Ridge Road. We hiked from Forest Canyon Overlook to the top of Mount Ida (12,889 feet) and back, a distance of about nine miles, all above tree line. We were basically following the ridge of the Continental Divide with fabulous views of the lakes, streams, and canyons below us. One of the most spectacular views was looking down on Arrowhead, Doughnut, Inkwell, Highest, and Azure lakes, all in the same dramatic gorge below Mount Julian. I added that gorge to my mental "yet to hike" list, but unfortunately, I was never able to check that one off. There was no formal trail to that destination, so it was not part of my three-year goal to hike all of the trails.

Afternoon thunderstorms were common in the mountains in the summer months, and it was best to be aware of approaching storms and the possibility of lightning. We were admiring the great views from the top of Mount Ida when a nearby thunderbolt startled us into action. The recommended defense was to put distance between yourself and others to lessen the chance of multiple injuries and to get off high points as quickly as possible. Noting that the hair on the back of our necks was standing up, an ominous sign, we separated and began moving downhill toward trees as fast as possible in the rugged terrain. There was no conversation, just action. Fortunately, the storm passed without further incident, but it instantly changed our priority for the afternoon.

Later that same summer, several visitors were seriously injured by lightning, and there were two fatalities. One victim had severe burns on the head and a burn hole in the sole of his shoe. The other victim had deep burns under the jewelry around her neck. Public messaging emphasizes the hazards and potential dangers as well as suggested safe practices to minimize the risk. When caught in the open with no way to reach safety, it is advised that hikers squat down, remaining on their tiptoes to lessen ground contact, and avoid being the tallest object around.

West Unit Manager Jock Whitworth on our climb up Mount Ida

— — — — — —

We told the many hikers planning to climb Longs Peak (14,259 feet) that they needed to start up the trail around 3 to 4 a.m., usually with headlamps, and to be sure to leave the summit by noon to avoid the afternoon thunderstorms that typically occurred in the mountains of Colorado. Storms approached from the west, and hikers and climbers were on the east side of Longs Peak, which obscured their view of any approaching storm and thereby increasing the danger. The climb to the summit from the Longs Peak Ranger Station is an arduous eight miles with an elevation gain of over 5,000 feet. The last portion in rugged terrain includes some ledges and a steep chute called the "Home Stretch."

One day, we had a search and rescue team on the Longs Peak Boulder Field (just below the more difficult section of trail leading to the summit) carrying a visitor with a broken leg in a basket litter. A surprise lightning storm was suddenly right above them having just blown across the top of the summit. With the hair on their necks standing up, indicating a possible imminent strike, they had to take fast action to minimize the danger. They got the patient out of the metal basket, took off any metal they had on their bodies, and put those items in the basket. Everyone then spread out among the boulders. As recommended, they squatted as low as they could, remaining on their tiptoes to minimize ground contact. Of course, this looked pretty odd to a nearby hiker who was unaware of the threat, so he approached the group asking, "What is going on?" Now he was the highest point around, almost a human lightning rod, so members of the team told him to "get away from us, spread out, and get down as low as you can go." He still seemed oblivious to the danger, so they repeatedly yelled, "Lightning!" pointing to the sky and "Get away from us and get down!" Fortunately, no one was hit, but it made for some tense moments and a little embarrassment on the part of the hiker from Ohio.

A Longmont, Colorado, man was not so lucky. He and a group of friends set out on a hike to the top of Longs Peak one summer day, but they got a very late start, nearly 9 a.m. By the time they got to the Chasm Lake Junction, a little over halfway to the top, dark clouds were overhead. The group discussed whether to turn back or change course. The Longmont man had recently bought his first cellphone, and he had told his wife at home that he would call her from the summit of Longs Peak, so he pleaded to go on. The group split, with some abandoning the original goal and heading to Chasm Lake instead. The remainder of the group continued toward the summit still over three miles away. By the time the summit group got to the Keyhole, where the going gets much more difficult with the "Narrows" and a steep rock gulley ahead, it was raining lightly. Some in the group again raised the concern over weather and the wisdom of going on, and all but two turned back. The Longmont man and a woman who decided to go with him to the top continued because he was determined to make that call. It was on the way down the steep gulley when the woman slipped on the wet rocks and almost fell, but was saved by the man who grabbed her arm. However, after pushing her to safety, he lost his balance and fell to his death. Bystanders below rushed to the man, but it was too late except to call the park rangers using the new cellphone.

Search and rescue (SAR) is an important role for park employees and involved highly trained rangers, educators, trail workers, and even administrative staff. These folks from all park departments volunteered to be called for SAR missions, and they attend various training sessions throughout the year. Typically, there were sixty to seventy-five SAR incidents annually, and of those twenty or more would be considered major, meaning they cost more than $5,000. Back then, helicopter time was around $500 to $600 per hour so a complex rescue could quickly run into the tens of thousands of dollars. Fortunately, the cost of the major SARs was paid for from a central fund and did not come from the park budget. Management needed to make the best decisions for a successful outcome, and with park budgets always inadequate, the central funding avoided having to make decisions based on cost rather than effectiveness.

Search and rescue (SAR) crews load an injured party
onto Lifeflight for a fast trip to the hospital.

101

Each year some of the more than 50 SARs in Rocky Mountain
NP involve high angle or technical rescue.

We used the national Incident Command System (ICS) to manage major
incidents in the park. The chief ranger would appoint an incident commander
(IC) to oversee the operation, which could last from hours to days depending
on the circumstances. The IC would appoint others to fill various key positions
on the team including planning, logistics, public information, and administration (payroll, purchasing emergency supplies, and food). Sometimes the IC
would set up at park headquarters, and sometimes they would be closer to the
scene. We also designated one ranger to act as liaison with family or friends
who were awaiting the outcome. This person could keep the anxious relatives
informed and provide other assistance as needed. Park dispatch was always a
key component since radio traffic was essential. During a major incident, all

other employees were asked to avoid using the radio for routine business. For many rescues, a wheeled litter could be used to transport the victim back to the trailhead and a waiting ambulance. In more remote or serious circumstances, a helicopter would be used.

Park dispatch would routinely call me when a major search and rescue was underway. It was good to be briefed on emergency responses and the circumstances involved. The area news media had radio scanners, and they would call me when they overheard talk of an emergency response. Sometimes I would head to the office or to the scene to observe, and sometimes I would go with the crews to help. I recall a couple of searches that lasted for two or three days, with some rescuers working through the night. At the end of each incident, there was a debriefing at headquarters, usually with food and drink provided.

Fatal accidents were always analyzed by the park staff during a board of inquiry, and key people involved in the incident were interviewed for the record. These important boards carefully review the circumstances of the accident, and the actions taken by first responders and other rescuers. The objective is to identify lessons learned and develop recommendations for ways to improve safety education, visitor information, and the park's response. We also review and try to improve efforts to inform visitors of safe practices and the need for sound judgment. Media coverage of fatalities and major rescues also provided opportunities for our staff to get important safety messages to the public. During my tenure at Rocky, we averaged three to four fatalities per year, with as many as ten in one year. On one hand, given several million visitors each year, we were lucky there were not more serious accidents. On the other hand, major search and rescues, and especially fatal accidents, were not only tragic for the family involved, but they took a toll on the park staff.

- - - - - -

One Saturday morning in June 1994, park dispatch called me at home to say there were three climbers stranded on 12,720-foot Hallett Peak. One in the party was climbing above the other two who were waiting on a ledge below. The lead climber un-roped, fell, and landed on his two climbing partners, which knocked one of the two off the narrow ledge. She fell some sixty feet to another ledge resulting in serious back injuries.

It would be a complex and challenging rescue, requiring numerous technical climbing rescuers and their equipment that would be flown to the top of Hallett Peak. The National Park Service contracts for helicopter service, and helicopter missions operate from Rocky's Hollowell Park helipad. The National Park Service provides a trained helicopter manager to oversee flight operations. It includes making weight calculations to determine the amount of personnel and equipment that can be safely carried on each flight. Working in and around helicopters can be dangerous, especially as you approach the copter with the rotors turning. They could literally take your head off, so people use extreme caution. Anyone who might fly in a helicopter had to take mandatory training, and they also were required to wear fire-resistant clothing, including gloves and a helmet during the flight.

Search and Rescue (SAR) crews await their flights to the
top of Hallet Peak for a complex rescue mission.

This particular operation required multiple flights to the top of Hallett Peak to position the required rescue personnel and equipment. Flights continued all afternoon. Unbeknownst to us, the pilot was anxious to get back to Fort Collins to see his daughter perform in a piano recital that evening. For the last flight of the day, the pilot loaded extra fuel to allow him to fly from the top of Hallett directly to Fort Collins in time for the recital. The park's helicopter manager did the calculations adding the weight of the fuel, equipment and two final rescuers and factored in the elevation at the top and the air temperature. She informed the pilot that he was overweight and needed to remove some fuel. He argued that he was not overweight, and as the pilot he would make the final determination. She objected, but he was adamant that it was his decision and he took off.

Approaching the top of the peak, the pilot lost control and the helicopter crashed on the rocky summit, spraying metal shrapnel from the rotor blades in all directions. It was fortunate that no one was seriously injured, but the helicopter was destroyed. Everyone spent the night on Hallett, and another helicopter finished the mission the following day. Rescuers go prepared with extra clothing and supplies in case the operation requires more time than anticipated. A larger helicopter had to fly the wreckage out in pieces. A board of inquiry found the pilot of the first helicopter to be at fault for the accident. In addition, rangers determined that the climbing party was not adequately skilled and experienced for the route chosen. Additionally, they had no map, no helmets, and no technical gear, and yet they were climbing a section that was above their skill level without the proper equipment.

Crashed helicopter on Hallet Peak – due to pilot
error. Fortunately no serious injuries.

Some search or rescue operations can take hours and even days. SAR team members usually report to the SAR cache to get the right equipment for the incident, such as climbing gear or the wheeled litter, to receive a briefing from the incident commander, and grab a few granola bars or other snack items to eat in lieu of meals once they get involved far from food and shelter. During some complex operations, we would have sandwiches and water delivered up the trail by volunteers. If SAR teams go without a meal or two while hard at work, we often would have pizza and other food waiting for them when they returned to headquarters.

— — — — — —

One weekend at home I turned on my park radio to monitor park operations on a typical busy summer day. As usual, radio traffic was heavy, and I was soon listening to an exchange between dispatch and some rangers in the field. I had missed the early parts of what seemed like an incident at Fern Lake, a popular hiking destination 4.5 miles from a trailhead. The exchange was something like this: Ranger to dispatch: "Where is Ranger Oliver?" Dispatch: "He is on his way." Ranger: "What is his ETA to Fern Lake?" Dispatch: "About ninety minutes." Ranger: "Does he have the item?" Dispatch: "Yes." By this time, I feared the worst: like a possible fatality (we often used code on the radio to avoid saying words like body bag. So, I telephoned dispatch to get briefed on the incident and learned that there was a district ranger meeting (four to five rangers) at the Fern Lake patrol cabin. When I asked what "item" they were referring to, I was told it was one of Laurie Oliver's outstanding peach pies! No wonder the concern and urgency.

– – – – – –

On another occasion, a Sunday afternoon in July of 1996, dispatch called to say they were involved in a major rescue operation on Longs Peak (14,259 feet), the highest mountain in the park. Furthermore, the injured party was a friend of mine, Nate Dick. Nate was 51 at the time and an experienced mountaineer in top shape. He usually hiked alone because most people could not keep up with him.

On this Sunday morning, Nate told his wife, Karen, that he was going to climb Mount Lady Washington at 13,281' elevation, and that he would call her from there with his new cellphone. Once on top of Lady Washington, he decided it was such a beautiful day that he would descend to the saddle. Rather than hiking down he would glissade down a couloir named Lambs Slide. A couloir is defined as a steep gully or gorge usually filled with snow or ice. Glissading is essentially a controlled slide down a snow chute using an ice ax as a brake to slow descent. Lambs Slide was named for the first person, Reverend Elkanah Lamb, to survive a fall the length of the couloir in 1871. Since then, most falls in this couloir have resulted in more tragic outcomes.

Lambs Slide is a steep, snow- and ice-covered couloir which drops over 1000 feet.

Nate tested the snow at the top of Lambs Slide to make sure it was not solid ice and that his ice ax would work for the essential braking action. The appropriate term is self-arresting with the ice ax. He pushed off for a short distance and tested it again, and he was satisfied it was safe to go. Within a few seconds after he pushed off for the shortcut to the bottom, he realized it was indeed solid ice and he was out of control in a fast fall down the ice chute. In flailing about trying to regain some control, the pointed end of the ice ax caught him in the neck puncturing his right subclavian artery. His out of control slide down the couloir ended in the rocks of Mills Glacier more than 1,000 feet below. Nate also sustained various injuries to his left hip, right clavicle, right elbow, neck, and ulnar nerve. Two nearby climbers saw his fall and worse yet the blood spurting from this neck wound. They were able to get to him quickly and render aid to save his life.

One of the climbers was able to significantly slow the arterial bleeding with direct pressure until relieved by park paramedic and climbing ranger Mike Pratt who also was in the area and arrived about thirty minutes later. A Rocky Mountain Rescue volunteer who rushed to assist found Nate's cellphone in his pocket and used it to quickly start the national park's emergency response.

The story of Nate's evacuation to a hospital in Denver is also extraordinary. A Flight for Life helicopter was unable to reach Mills Glacier due to strong winds but did shuttle rescue personnel and supplies to near Chasm Lake. Ranger Dan Ostrowski and a litter team lowered Nate over 800 feet in four 200-foot lowering actions, including three on ice and snow, and one on scree (loose rock) to get him near Chasm Lake below. Wind still prevented the helicopter from landing, but fortunately, Rick Guerrieri, the incident commander, had initiated a backup plan. He sent Ranger Scott Hall to run up to Chasm Lake (a distance of 4.2 miles with an elevation gain of 2,398 feet) in approximately 45 minutes carrying a sixty-five-pound raft on his back – an amazing feat. The raft was inflated and paddled across Chasm Lake to bring Nate back across the water. By that time, winds had subsided enough to allow a helicopter to pick up Nate and fly him to a Denver hospital. The surgeon said Nate's injuries were technically "non-survivable." No doubt, the proximity of skilled people, their fast action, and the amazing response of the Rocky Mountain National Park SAR team, plus a good deal of luck, made the difference. Nate is back to mountain climbing and hiking, but more glissading is probably out.

‒ ‒ ‒ ‒ ‒ ‒

One Monday morning, rangers reported an unusual event over the weekend. A forty-two-year-old man was climbing alone on Taylor Glacier. Near the top of the 1,400-foot hardpack snow and ice gully, he fell to his death. When rangers got to the scene, they observed that all his clothing and equipment appeared like new. In his pocket was a note that said, "In the event of my death, please notify XXX funeral home in Boulder." When rangers contacted the funeral home, the owner said, "I remember that guy and we have a file that he left here." Looking at the file, there was a sample obituary written as if this person had died in a rafting accident. It all seemed strange. After further investigation, rangers concluded that the individual, a librarian by vocation, liked to read outdoor adventure books and then experience the activity; hence the new clothing and equipment. He must have assumed that one day it might catch up to him – and it did.

‒ ‒ ‒ ‒ ‒ ‒

Nearing the end of my goal of hiking all of the park's trails, I had one long, difficult hike remaining. I was afraid it was more than my wife, Barb, would want to undertake. So, I asked around the office and Ranger Vicki offered to go along. This hike was about twenty-two miles beginning at Bear Lake, going up and over Flattop Mountain (12,324 feet), down the other side of the Continental Divide, and out to Green Mountain trailhead on the west side of the park. Along the way, we had to take a 1.5-mile spur trail to Haynach Lakes (in order to complete that segment), then take the Tonahutu Creek Trail to Big Meadows, and finish with a segment of the Green Mountain Trail. In the end, Barb came along, which almost resulted in divorce (not really, just some serious discontent).

First of all, I knew Barb would not like twenty-two miles in one day, so I shaved a few off my estimate, which didn't go over too well since she also had a map. Secondly and more significant was something I found out later, and that was Ranger Vicki was called "the animal" because no one could keep up with her hiking and she never stopped. It was no wonder that I was struggling to stay with her and inadvertently leaving my wife farther and farther behind. We waited for Barb to catch up at the Haynach Lakes junction, and she quickly convinced me that I should be hiking with her and not Vicki. My wife's telling of this story gets better with time, but it is a hike neither of us will forget. It was a long day in several respects.

We made an earlier attempt at this long hike over Flattop Mountain and on to Grand Lake, but it was fall and weather was a concern. We hiked the 4.5 miles to the top of Flattop, with an elevation gain of 2,877 feet. It would have been all downhill from there, but once on top, strong winds and snow flurries made us turn back without finishing that hike. Weather is obviously one critical factor when making decisions in the mountains any time of year. There was a saying among park staff: "The mountains don't care, we do!"

I didn't quite complete all of the trails in three years, but I came close. I only had one remaining hike at the beginning of my fourth summer. The last hike to meet my goal was a segment that went from the park's northwest corner to Corral Creek, a distance of about twenty miles. I asked Jock Whitworth, the district manager, to hike with me to Corral Creek where we would meet my wife with a car to drive us back. The hike went some thirteen miles to the top of Comanche Peak (12,702 feet) and then another seven miles down into Corral Creek. The view of Mirror Lake from the top of Comanche Peak was spectacular. Another long hike but well worth it. It was now time for a new pair of hiking boots.

- - - - - -

Most employees carry a park radio when they are in the park, and many (like me) carry them when off duty in the park in order to assist visitors when called upon. Ranger Barry Sweet was hiking alone one day in uniform and talking to visitors as much as possible. He overheard radio traffic between dispatch and Kurt Oliver, the district ranger. It seemed a hiker had jumped a small ravine and jammed his knee and was unable to walk without great pain. The hiker's location was reported as above Andrew's Glacier just below Taylor Peak (13,153 feet). If a ranger hiked from the nearest trailhead it would be at least two hours before help could arrive. Ranger Barry was about thirty minutes away and he let dispatch know of his location in case he could help. They advised him he was closer than Ranger Kurt and that he should head over that way to assess the situation. He arrived at the upper end of Andrews Glacier, the ridge below Hallett, but there was no one there. He saw several people at the bottom of the snowfield about 300 yards below. He figured that those must be the folks in need of help.

Hikers carefully make their way down Andrews
Glacier from Hallet Peak to Andrews Tarn.

He was wearing an NPS parka, and took that off and placed it on the snow. He sat on it and pulled it up between his legs. He was going to slide down the glacier using his boots to slow his descent. He traveled the length of the snowfield quickly in stages stopping enough to make sure he remained in control. The last fifty yards or so he slid toward the group, stopped, and said, "Did someone call for a ranger?" He startled the group because they were expecting someone to come from below them rather than from above. They wanted to know if he lived up there? He went on to assist them in moving slowly toward the main trail. When crossing snowfields, Barry would pull the injured man along on his makeshift sled, his parka. After a couple of hours of slow progress, they met another ranger coming up the trail with a mule to take the man down to the trailhead. All in a day's work.

Our dedicated and highly skilled rangers often worked in difficult circumstances and at significant personal risk in order to rescue climbers, hikers, and others who get into trouble. We had one individual who had to be rescued three times in one week, a park record. All three situations involved carelessness or poor judgment. After the third rescue, rangers issued him a citation for disorderly conduct that required a court appearance before a federal magistrate. The judge fined the man to recover some of the rescue costs and banned him from the park for a year, preventing further rescues of him, at least for a while.

— — — — — —

In addition to search and rescue work, we used helicopters for management purposes, including backcountry projects requiring the transportation of equipment and personnel. One such project was the Bluebird Lake dam removal and restoration at nearly 11,000 feet elevation and 6.3 miles from the nearest trailhead.

By way of background, in 1982 the Lawn Lake dam high in the park broke, flooded the town of Estes Park, and killed three people. There likely would have been more fatalities if it were not for early warning sounded by a man collecting trash at the Lawn Lake trailhead who heard the roar and called police. The creek running down the gorge was appropriately named Roaring River. As a result of the Lawn Lake dam failure, other private dams within national parks were checked and a condition assessment was written for each.

One such dam was the Bluebird Lake dam, constructed in 1903, which was found to be in poor condition due to lack of maintenance. The reinforced concrete dam was about 200 feet long on top and fifty-five feet high at the highest point. It took two years (1989-90) to fully break-up and remove the structure. To begin the demolition, a front-end loader and an excavator had to be flown in by Army Chinook helicopter furnished by Fort Carson in Colorado. Even with a heavy lift capacity Chinook, the equipment had to be transported in pieces and then reassembled at the work site. The first summer, crews worked to tear down the structure and separate rubble into piles of concrete and rebar. Crews worked four and a half ten-hour days, living in tents and eating meals prepared by a cook in the cook shack, a small stone building left at the site after construction of the dam. At the end of the four-day shift, the crew would be flown out, and that day another crew would be flown in. The work season was short due to the elevation and mountain weather.

Steve Iobst, the chief of maintenance, and I flew up to the work site one morning to check on progress and talk to the crew. As we landed, I noticed a big guy, appropriately named Thor, sitting on a rock eating a sandwich. I said, "It seems a little early for lunch, doesn't it, Thor?" It was barely 8 a.m. and he replied that it wasn't lunch, just a snack. He said he'd usually eat seven or eight sandwiches a day, but given the hard work and long hours there was no worry about gaining weight.

Others on the crew told the story of Thor wanting to go to a chili cook-off at an employee's house in the nearby town of Allenspark, but he worked that day. So at the end of his shift he hiked down the six miles to the trailhead, rode his bike another five miles to the chili feed, enjoyed the evening's food and drink, rode the bike back to the trailhead, and hiked back up to the camp in time to get a couple of hours of sleep before starting work at 6 o'clock next morning. Thor evidently liked chili – a lot.

The second season of the project was mostly focused on removing the piles of debris and doing the final cleanup to allow the natural environment to heal on its own. How to get the tons of concrete rubble and the steel rebar from the dam site to a disposal area was debated for some time. Using a team of mules was one option. It was determined that the mule train would have done extensive damage to the trail and cost nearly as much as flying the material out. In the end, we hired a Sikorski Sky Crane (aptly named "The Incredible Hulk"), which was capable of lifting 10,000 pounds at 10,000 feet elevation. The crane came from Oregon inside a cargo plane (in two pieces), then reassembled in Loveland and flown to the park. It took multiple trips flying from the temporary base inside the park, up to the lake and back over a four-day period. Crews had built two special containers for flying the debris out, so one could be loaded while the other was being flown down to the base and dumped. Trucks would then be filled to haul it off to a waste disposal site. Over the course of those four days, the Sky Crane flew 1,100 tons (or 2.2 million pounds) of debris from Bluebird Lake to the Wild Basin transfer site. The chief of maintenance told me that the nearly $500,000 dollar purchase order for the helicopter was the largest purchase order he signed in his career. Like most boys, our son, Chris, about 12 at the time, was fascinated by heavy equipment and especially helicopters. My wife dropped him off at the base of operations with a lawn chair and sack lunch where he sat all day watching the giant helicopter come and go. I am sure it was the highlight of his summer.

Previous page: turning the Bluebird Dam into rubble to be
flown out by the heavy lift Sikorsky Sky Crane (above).

— — — — — —

I had many occasions to drive from headquarters outside of Estes Park to
Kawuneeche Visitor Center, some forty-five miles across Trail Ridge Road on
the park's west side. No matter how many times I did it, I always enjoyed the
spectacular mountain views and abundant wildlife, and seeing all of the people
enjoying Rocky Mountain National Park. On one drive across, I came to a
pickup truck in the middle of one lane with both doors open and the motor
running but no driver in sight. I stopped with my flashers on and got out to
look down over the side of the road. Sure enough, there was a man and his son
about a hundred feet from the road, taking pictures of a great bull elk on the
tundra. I said, "Excuse me, sir, your truck is blocking traffic." And he replied
as he gave me a shrug, "Sorry, I am on vacation," as if he had left his common
sense at home. I am sure his photos of the handsome elk were shown with
pride back home.

In the mountains, it is always possible to get a snowstorm even in the summer. One Fourth of July, we had to close Trail Ridge Road due to heavy snow. Some folks from Estes Park drove over to Grand Lake on the west side to watch fireworks and then could not get back without going the long way around. That meant a trip of three hours instead of one. We would also temporarily close Trail Ridge Road because of dense fog that would develop so fast there would still be cars having to drive through it. I have seen cars hugging the centerline, and a few driving on or left of the line, most likely to avoid getting too close to the edge. There are many places along the road where there are sheer drop-offs of hundreds of feet or more.

Unfortunately, one year, two young men in a big Chevy Suburban missed a turn in the fog and drove over the edge. Their car was a ball of junk after tumbling some 1,000 feet or more down a steep rocky slope. Pulling the car up with cable from a heavy-duty wrecker truck loosened several large boulders that increased in speed as they rolled downhill. I saw one bounce and land in a dense stand of trees which seemed to loudly explode on impact. The trees were reduced to toothpicks.

On another trip across Trail Ridge, I saw a motorcycle with a side car coming at me from the other direction. The driver was in a blue coat and blue helmet. Oddly, the person in the side car was wearing a fur coat, red scarf, and goggles. That person turned out to be a large brown dog sitting up straight, enjoying the views through those nice goggles. I wish I had taken a photo of that colorful duo touring Colorado.

— — — — —

Early one morning, one of our west side rangers came upon a pickup truck with Oklahoma plates resting on its side next to the road in a ditch. He walked up to the vehicle and noticed a man standing upright on the passenger door with his head behind the steering wheel. As he approached, the man said, "I am glad to see you." After determining that the man was not injured, the ranger helped him climb out of the truck and asked him what happened. The man said he had fallen asleep at the wheel and driven off the road sometime after midnight, and he was too afraid to get out. The ranger asked, "Afraid of what?" and the man replied, "Bears, man, bears!"

Injuries from wildlife are rare in Rocky Mountain since there are no grizzly bears or poisonous snakes. In an extremely rare case, there was one deadly encounter with a mountain lion that attacked a lone runner. That tragic incident resulted in several management actions, including posting of warning signs, increased visitor education on how to prevent lion encounters, and what to do if a lion is spotted.

A few years earlier, a park employee had a close call with a mountain lion in the same general area. The woman regularly jogged a six-mile loop after work that included a one-mile section of trail along the side of Big Meadow. The woman was tall and strong from years of working on the park's trail crew. On this particular day as she ran down the side of Big Meadow, she was suddenly overcome with what she called a "very bad feeling" and sense of "impending doom." As she turned her head to look behind her, she saw a mountain lion in the air about to land on her back. She quickly raised her arms in a defensive posture, catching the lion on her forearms, and with a rush of adrenaline, she was able to throw it off. Grabbing a nearby tree limb, she used it to threaten the animal and discourage the lion from further attack. It slowly wandered off, probably in search of other prey. With scratched arms and in some shock, she hurried down the trail toward her car and safety. Research indicates that a lone jogger moving at dusk in mountain lion habitat can trigger the predator/prey response, as in this case.

- - - - - -

We did experience another unusual visitor-wildlife encounter one day when a rodeo rider and his friend were traveling through the park on their motorcycles. Seeing some magnificent bull elk in a nearby meadow, the rodeo guy (calf wrestler and bull rider) thought he would like to try his hand at elk wrestling. So, he got on the back of his friend's motorcycle, and they rode off into the meadow after a bull. He did make the jump from the cycle to the elk but was immediately thrown off just as a park ranger drove up, responding to phone calls from concerned visitors. Citations were issued for harassing wildlife and driving off road. Later, park staff decided it was probably the first case of "catch and release" elk hunting – and hopefully the last.

– – – – – –

One morning while walking through Moraine Park Campground (in uniform) observing visitor use and talking to a few campers, I noticed two small boys, about four and six, chasing a baby bird around the trunk of a tree. I went over to them and said, "Boys, boys. Please don't chase that bird; it hasn't learned to fly yet." The fast thinking older boy said, "I know, we're trying to teach it,"

– – – – – –

Rangers often made snowmobile patrols of the park boundary in winter, and I sometimes went along. The most common route was to follow the Long Draw Road (closed in winter) and trails to the Corral Creek patrol cabin some twelve miles from the highway. The cabin was at one end of the Long Draw Reservoir, which was iced over and then covered in snow. Snowmobiling in deep snow was like being in a sugar bowl. Maintaining momentum and staying on the tracks of the lead snowmobile was important. Not as experienced as our rangers, I became the problem child, tipping over into deep snow several times on the trip. It then took at least two people to wrestle the snowmobile back onto the track while standing in deep snow with little solid footing.

Once at the cabin, we usually had to dig our way through deep snow to get into the porch for access to the door. A snow shovel was hung in a tree near the cabin to be accessible even with a lot of snow on the ground.

Backcountry patrol cabins were always prepared and ready for the next visitor in case there was an urgent need for shelter and warmth. The water jugs were full of snow for melting, and the wood stove laid with firewood and kindling with matches nearby for a fast start. Deep snow also covered the metal roof and once the interior of the cabin was heated up, all the snow on the roof would slide off. It was important not to park your snowmobile in the wrong place, or you would have to dig to find it. It was also important to keep the shovel inside so it would not be lost under snow.

Winter patrols along the boundary like this looked for problems, with particular attention to possible poaching of wildlife inside the park. To get a better view of surrounding meadows and hillsides, we would snowmobile up the side of a mountain and then post hole (sinking in with each step) across the snow-covered slope to a viewpoint on the other side. From there we could see a vast area in the valley below. We struggled across 200 yards or more of deep snow on the slope for the best view. Before returning across the slope, the district ranger cautioned us to spread out because of the potential for avalanches. Having just crossed that slope already and now needing to cross over again, I said, "Now you tell me!" Deep snow, especially on layers of hard pack or ice, significantly increased the risk. Needless to say, I was glad to safely reach the other side.

— — — — — —

Being a park superintendent or deputy is indeed a great job. However, sometimes we had to deal with public controversy, and at times it could get a bit ugly. I remember when Superintendent Jim Thompson wore a bulletproof vest to a public meeting, and we had a couple of armed rangers in the audience. This unusual precaution was the result of the park's proposal to close a small ski area inside the park. The ski area was failing, it was not sustainable, natural snowfall was declining, and there was no water to make snow. At least one individual was very vocal, and he fought hard to keep the ski area open despite the problems. At times, he came across as confrontational and potentially threatening. The superintendent announced our final decision at this crowded meeting in Estes Park. Fortunately, there was no incident. Soon after that public announcement, a contract heavy lift helicopter was hired to remove and fly out the ski lift towers to assure the decision was final.

— — — — — —

Ride the Rockies is an annual bike tour that crosses the state on a different route each summer. The ride organizers were eager to have the tour go through Rocky Mountain National Park, both for the scenic qualities and for the marketing value. Each year they would ask if the route could include Trail Ridge Road through the national park. We had politely declined citing various concerns, including disruption to other visitors, traffic problems with cars trying to pass the many bikes on narrow roads, and the potential for wildlife conflicts. Trail Ridge Road has no road shoulders, and because it was on the National Register of Historic Places, we would not consider widening the road. Organizers said the 2,500 bikes would ride in single file, and they would be up and out of the park by 10 a.m. when visitor traffic increases. To assure an early start, the organizers promised to make breakfast at dawn and announce that the luggage truck would be closed at 7 a.m. to force riders to stick to the tighter schedule for that morning. We decided to allow it as a trial run.

On the day of the ride, park managers observed from a variety of locations along the route. We agreed to take notes and identify any problems from the large numbers of bike riders. It was quickly obvious that promises were hard to keep. The hundreds of cyclists were spread out in one constant moving mass with riders consistently ignoring the single file directive. That wasn't realistic with the number of bikes. Cyclists were usually five abreast, and there were few breaks in the stream of riders. They consistently consumed one lane, making it difficult for two-way traffic to travel through the park during the event.

Over 2,000 riders completed the 47 mile Ride the Rockies trip through Rocky Mountain NP but disruption to auto traffic was greater than anticipated.

I was standing at the beginning of Horseshoe Park, a large meadow area where elk and bighorn sheep are often observed. Sure enough, there was a group of twenty-five or so elk, including some mature bulls with large racks in the meadow on the other side of the road. When elk are stressed, they raise their heads and nervously prance around in a circular motion. The large number and steady stream of bikes made it impossible for the elk to cross the road. The elk made several attempts to cross the road only to turn back with their heads held high. We decided to stop the bike riders and let the elk cross. We held up the bikes for about five minutes, and the herd of elk with their fresh summer coats finally crossed the road. A woman in the front of the riders said "Wow, that was so cool! Are those reindeer?"

The other problem I saw was where the Continental Divide crossed Trail Ridge Road (Milner Pass at 10,759 feet elevation) and also at the high point of the road (just over 12,000 feet). Both places had large park signs to identify these significant points along Trail Ridge Road. Many of the riders wanted their photo taken with the signs as background as they held their bikes over their heads, probably to prove they made it. Large crowds gathered at both signs as they waited their turn, which neither organizers nor park managers antici-pated. My fifteen-year-old son, Chris, was among those waiting for his picture, although he was not an official participant in the entire five-day ride.

— — — — — —

Occasionally, our family would pack up and camp for the weekend in Moraine Park Campground or Timber Creek Campground on the other side. It was great fun to walk the campground and see all of the families enjoying Rocky Mountain National Park and nature. We also enjoyed getting away for a couple of days, hiking and sitting around the evening campfire. While at our campsite one morning, a large RV from Iowa pulled into the campsite across from ours. While the father got out to level the RV, I heard the kids yelling from inside: "Turn the generator on, Dad. Turn the generator on; we want to play video games." This chorus kept up for several minutes. It was all I could do to refrain from going over and telling them what they were missing. I wanted to say, "Come out here for a minute and take a look around. Do they have mountains like this in Iowa? See those dots out there in the meadow? Those are elk." I wanted to say they could have stayed home and played video games in the RV parked in their driveway and saved all that gasoline.

— — — — — —

There were several backcountry patrol cabins in the park, and employees could sign up to use them for a night or two as long as rangers were not scheduled to use them for official purposes. Backcountry cabins had emergency food and water, a wood stove, propane lamps, and other supplies, but non-official users were instructed to bring their own food and bedding. All cabin users were asked to take a park radio in case they needed to contact dispatch for visitor assistance or in an emergency. Each cabin had a logbook, and users would record their visit and something about their experience. We loved to read about the many great experiences of those folks that had been there before us.

I had heard such good things about the Thunder Lake patrol cabin, I reserved it for two nights for our family. It was 7.5 miles of trail with a steady climb until we reached Thunder Lake, which was a dramatic setting at the edge of the lake surrounded by towering peaks. The rustic log cabin was described as small but able to sleep four with a sleeping loft.

Our son was fifteen and our daughter thirteen, and we arrived at the cabin about 3 p.m. We unlocked the cabin and entered the small living space. There was a fold-up double bed on the main floor and sleep pads on the loft floor where our kids were going to sleep. Our daughter climbed the ladder to the loft and immediately announced, "I am not sleeping here!" I asked why not, and she said there is "mouse poop everywhere." I said we will clean it up, and there is nowhere else to sleep. She repeated, "I am not sleeping here tonight." Trying to be logical, I reminded her that our car was 7.5 miles away. What's more, we only had about three hours of light left, hoping to convince her of staying. She said, "Well, we had better get going then." Once it was apparent, we could not change her mind, we locked the cabin and headed back down the trail. We hiked the many miles back to our car a little after dark, using flashlights to find our way at the end. We could have insisted on staying at the cabin, but the threat of hantavirus was real at the time, and I figured it was not worth the argument or the risk.

— — — — — —

As fall approached, our road crews would place tall poles (lodgepole pine tree trunks) some as high as fifteen feet all along the highway (Trail Ridge Road – the highest continuously paved highway in the country with the high point of 12,183 feet). The purpose was to mark the edges of the road where snow drifts covered the highway, sometimes twenty feet deep or more. Snowplow operators could then confidently find the road without driving over a cliff. Plow operators worked ten- to twelve-hour days, four days a week, usually beginning in mid-April, to open the road between Estes Park and Grand Lake, a distance of forty-eight miles. These rotary plows could throw the snow a hundred feet or more, and crews would work from both ends until they met in the middle. Some days were whiteout conditions, and the operators only worked as long as they could see the road's yellow centerline between the cab and the rotary head, a space of about twelve inches. They called this "pulling the centerline." If the yellow line suddenly disappeared, they could be in imminent danger. Unfortunately, many years ago there had been at least one serious accident where a plow went off the edge, killing the operator.

Top: Rotary plows work for weeks to clear Trail Ridge Road and open buried buildings such as the Alpine Visitor Center (bottom).

Visitors wait in line for restrooms that are still mostly buried by snow.

The goal was to get one lane open between the two towns, and then they would widen that opening until this world-famous highway could be opened to two-way traffic. The target date was always Memorial Day weekend, and the town of Grand Lake depended on this to jumpstart its short tourist season. Residents of Grand Lake and Estes Park always complained that the road was slow to open. The problem was at the elevation of these towns, about 8,500 feet, the roads were free of snow much earlier than at 11,000 or 12,000 feet. Drifts could be fifteen to twenty feet high in places. To convince people of the work involved to open the road, we offered free bus tours to the work site on each side. Once shop owners appreciated the depth of the problem, they soon told others of the challenges the road crews faced, and we received fewer phone calls.

My last winter at Rocky Mountain was a milder than normal winter right up until early April. Snowpack in the mountains (important for summer water) was measured, and the results published as a percent of normal, with normal being a ten-year running average. At the beginning of April, the snowpack in Rocky that winter was around 80 percent of normal, which was below average. We anticipated an early opening of Trail Ridge Road because there would be less snow to plow. We were surprised when heavy snow began to fall for days on end throughout the month. By the end of April, snowpack was now more than 200 percent of normal, and it was going to be a challenge to open the road by Memorial Day as expected.

I decided to check on progress about a week before Memorial Day and drove up to the Alpine Visitor Center and Trail Ridge Store. Plows had opened one lane to that point. The established procedure for using the one lane that was open was to radio dispatch and advise them of direction of travel and then to let them know when we arrived at our destination. That way, there was no chance of meeting a vehicle coming the other way – a problem given there was no way to pass each other. When I arrived at the Alpine Visitor Center parking lot, I was amazed at what I saw.

Drifts of snow went to the peak of the store's roof and almost covered the visitor center completely. I could and did walk right to the peak of the roof. Crews had begun bulldozing access to the doors of the buildings. The operators of Trail Ridge Store hired college students to dig tunnels into the windows to get light into their building. The restroom in the parking lot was completely buried, and crews had dug a tunnel to the doors so they could be used.

Above: Road side drifts can be 20 feet high or more.

Large patches of snow remained through most of the summer to the delight of kids from lower elevations. Family snowball fights were a normal occurrence in July and even into August that year.

In the early summer, road crews would remove the snow poles and store them for a few months before they put them back again. One day in late spring while I was at the Alpine Visitor Center parking lot (in uniform as usual), a gentleman in a car with Florida plates drove up and rolled down his window. He asked if we flew flags on all of those poles along the road and said that must be "really pretty." I explained that they were snow poles and why they were so important. Embarrassed, he said, "Oh, of course," while I imagined crews of employees raising and lowering flags each day on hundreds of snow poles.

- - - - - -

Long lines formed daily at the small restroom at Bear Lake, one of the most popular destinations in the park. The parking lot fills early every day. To serve more people without long lines, park management decided to build a new, much larger vault toilet. With no running water, sewage had to be hauled away weekly by pumper truck. The new building would have twelve individual compartments, each with a locking door to allow either men or women to use them. Each toilet had a metal riser and metal toilet seat to reduce maintenance costs. One summer day, the new building was hit by lightning, which evidently blew a woman off one of the metal seats. She came running out (at least as fast as she could with her hiking pants around her ankles) and screamed, "What the HELL was THAT?" A ranger sitting on a metal-rimmed desk in the adjacent office also received a bit of a shocking experience as the metal edge burned her legs. In addition, she reported that there were numerous small burn holes on the papers on her desk. Fortunately, there were no serious injuries, just frayed nerves and good stories to tell.

To build that larger restroom building in the right place, a huge boulder had to be removed. It was too big to move with heavy equipment so our explosives expert, Jim Leons, the park roads foreman, was called in to break the rock into manageable pieces. After observing, from a safe distance, I told Jim that the blast was impressive, and I asked if that was the largest thing he had blown up. He surprised me by saying "No, the largest thing was a whale." I said, "Tell me that story," and he did. When he worked at Olympic National Park in Washington, a fifty-foot dead whale washed up on the beach. As the tides rose and fell, the whale would wash out and then back in over the course of a couple of weeks. One day a young boy climbed up on it and fell into the now rotten whale carcass. After the boy was rescued – and cleaned up – the superintendent told Jim, "I don't care what you do, but get rid of that whale so it's not coming back." Continuing his story, Jim said, "Ninety-eight pounds of well-placed TNT and it was bird food."

— — — — — —

Permanent workers often transfer between parks, and it doesn't take long before you have NPS friends at parks all over the country. As a relatively small agency, it is easy to reconnect with people you have either worked with before or meet others who know your friends at a particular park. It was always possible that you could end up working for someone that once worked for you. In addition, many employees live in the park housing area in the larger national parks, so folks not only work together they often socialize together. It is often described as one large family environment. There is also the common bond resulting from dedication to the purpose and mission of the national parks, and the rewarding career serving the American public in beautiful surroundings.

— — — — — —

National parks have always attracted great numbers of visitors including some dignitaries. We occasionally had important people such as members of Congress, governors, or Supreme Court justices in the park – some on official business, some on vacation. Several times members of Congress who had responsibility for Department of the Interior appropriations or oversight would come for an official visit. I appreciated them taking the time to visit a national park and learn about the important issues that Congress could help us deal with more effectively.

Two particularly noteworthy dignitaries were Pope John Paul II and the emperor and empress of Japan. In 1993, during his visit to Colorado for World Youth Day, Pope John Paul II prayed and blessed the Chapel on the Rock as part of his two days of rest and relaxation at Camp Saint Malo in Allenspark, just south of Estes Park. This was the biggest thing to ever happen at Camp Saint Malo, a small Catholic youth camp on the edge of Rocky Mountain National Park. The staff at Camp Saint Malo immediately began to prepare for the Pope's visit by painting the buildings inside and out. Volunteers under the direction of a well-known gardener added new flower gardens out front as a colorful welcome to the pontiff. As a head of state (the Vatican), the Pope was afforded all of the status and protection you might expect for the president of the United States. In fact, the Pope was to be transported to Camp Saint Malo via presidential helicopter, complete with a Blackhawk escort and Secret Service protection on the ground. Because the Pope wanted to have quiet time and a walk inside the national park, our chief ranger and staff were intimately involved in planning and on the ground protection during his visit. Planning took several weeks of meetings, with every detail being worked out in advance.

The day before the official arrival, all of those involved in planning went to Camp Saint Malo for a dress rehearsal, complete with the helicopters making a familiarization flight from Denver to the camp. Chief Ranger Joe Evans and I went to Camp Saint Malo to review final plans and to see the presidential helicopter make its practice landing on the parking lot in front of the camp's administration building. The new, elaborate flower gardens with colorful designs looked terrific lining the parking lot and the walkway to the building where the Pope would stay. The gardens, along with fresh paint and a thorough cleaning, made the camp sparkle in the dramatic mountain setting.

Soon the sound of approaching helicopters got everyone's attention. We were standing around the parking lot, but leaving plenty of room for the largest aircraft to land, although only momentarily before heading back to Denver for the night. The first helicopter was the Blackhawk gunship, which swooped in and out without landing. The huge presidential helicopter was next, and as it hovered above the parking lot and slowly landed, a tornado of flowers and peat moss was suddenly engulfing us. There was nowhere to hide from the blizzard of dirt and debris. I was uncomfortable all afternoon with dirt and peat that ended up inside my clothing from the tremendous rotor wash of the powerful aircraft.

The Pope is considered a Head of State and was brought
to the park in the Presidential helicopter.

No sooner had the helicopter lifted off for Denver when a dozen gardeners and helpers were out collecting flowers and plants to repair the damaged gardens. We thought it was not only impossible to recreate the intricate designs in a few hours, but the same outcome likely would occur the next day. However, the camp director said hopefully the Pope would see them from the air before the helicopter was low enough to destroy them again.

Local boy scouts gave the Pope some white tennis shoes with yellow laces for his walk in the park. Of course, Secret Service agents and rangers were stationed along the path. They were out of sight not only during his walk, but for hours beforehand to assure his safety and solitude. The charismatic Pope even ventured out to the roadblocks to say hello to the crowd waiting in hopes of getting a glimpse of the pontiff.

Unfortunately, a fire destroyed the retreat center in 2011, and since then, Camp Saint Malo has remained closed. In 2013, one hundred-year rains produced flooding and mudslides, which destroyed the natural terrain and camp property, including the historic Pope John Paul II Trail named in honor of his visit. The Chapel on the Rock was undamaged, but due to the surrounding landscape damage, it has only been occasionally open to the public. The Archdiocese of Denver recently announced plans to preserve the beauty and rich history of the Chapel on the Rock and the Pope Saint John Paul II Trail. In addition, they plan to build a new visitor center nearby. The future of the camp itself is still uncertain.

- - - - - -

The following summer, in June of 1994, Emperor Akihito and Empress Michiko of Japan visited Rocky, but not before several busloads of Japanese ambassadors, Japanese Secret Service and U.S. Secret Service came to park headquarters to plan every detail. At the final planning meeting, the Japanese delegation wanted to see the room where the visit would take place, and they wanted to see the chairs where they would sit. Representatives also asked if a gift would be presented to which we replied that we intended to give them a framed photograph of Bear Lake. The lead planner asked to see the gift and then pulled a tape measure from his pocket so he could record the exact measurements of the large photograph. The planners also insisted that the building restrooms be available only to the royal party for the day of the visit, and that meant we had to arrange for portable toilets for everyone else.

It all started because the emperor's son had visited Bear Lake and had recommended that his father see it when in the U.S. In addition, the empress wanted to see alpine wildflowers but, in the end, neither objective was met. The planners felt that alpine wildflowers were at too high an elevation for a safe visit by the empress, and they were also afraid that closing popular Bear Lake during the official visit would be a public relations problem. Japanese advance planners decided to settle for a brief tour by motorcade and a naturalist talk at the Moraine Park Museum with its large picture window and great views of the beautiful mountain scenery. As naturalist Jean Muenchrath spoke, the emperor and empress each had their own translator whispering in their ear. Each translator had an English-Japanese dictionary with one in the form of a traditional small book while the other used a hand-held electronic device most assuredly made in Japan.

Had the motorcade arrived on schedule, afternoon thunderstorms would not have been a problem. However, they were more than an hour late, and as the motorcade entered the park, it was pouring rain with thunder in the distance. Following protocol was important, so as prearranged, the superintendent was to meet the emperor and empress at the curb and escort them into the building. As deputy superintendent, I was to meet the Japanese ambassador to the United States at the curb and escort him into the building.

As the motorcade entered the parking lot, the superintendent and I opened the door and opened our umbrellas to walk to the curb in the pouring rain. The Japanese Secret Service stopped us and said emphatically, "No umbrellas, no umbrellas!" and pointed to the sky and said "Lightning, lightning." Given that our uniform hats are straw and not at all waterproof, we reluctantly left the umbrellas in the building and walked into the rain to await the royal party.

134

As the emperor began to step out of his limousine, he put up his umbrella and gave us a funny look, probably thinking, "Are you guys crazy? It is pouring rain!" Our soaked and drooping straw hats were now ruined.

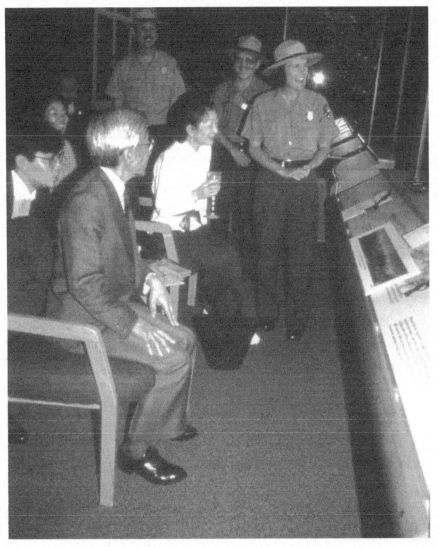

Emperor and Empress of Japan at the Moraine Park Museum.

After the naturalist talk and some light refreshments, the emperor and empress returned to their limousines again under their umbrellas. Within less than a minute of the motorcade leaving the parking lot, a strong bolt of lightning exploded a large tree at the edge of the pavement. Everyone exchanged astonished glances, and we thought maybe the Japanese Secret Service was right after all.

Fortunately, the rain subsided long enough for the empress to stop at a small pond where bighorn sheep often gather. After hearing the story of the sheep crossing the road to get to the pond, the empress said she wanted to "run, like the sheep" as she hurried to the sheep's mineral lick from the nearby road. The unplanned stop sent both the Japanese and U.S. Secret Service personnel scrambling to cordon off the area. It was fun to see the emperor taking photos of the empress with his Instamatic camera as she walked back to the road from the small pond, just like many regular tourists would do. It was another memorable day in the life of park rangers.

We always breathed a sigh of relief once dignitaries left the park, glad that there weren't any problems to mar the visit. These high-profile visits meant an increase in publicity and a corresponding bump in the numbers of park visitors. That caused both advantages and disadvantages. The most popular national parks like Rocky tended to get priority during budget negotiations in Washington. On the other hand, high visitation numbers for parks often meant overcrowding at peak times, and this presented a significant challenge for park managers.

— — — — — —

With nearly three million visitors per year, we received some interesting letters from those planning a visit to the park and amusing questions from people already there.

One of the common questions at the Trail Ridge Information center at 11,796 feet was "Where is the restroom?" My favorite was "Where am I, and where am I going?" This is a question that one might like to answer by saying, "If you don't know, how would you expect me to know?" but we would never do that. People would drive up and over Trail Ridge Road between Grand Lake and Estes Park, 48 miles of very scenic mountain highway. It could be slow with many curves, sometimes heavy traffic, and sometimes bad weather including snow or fog. When they arrived at the Alpine Visitor Center, the highest visitor center in the National Park System, often tired and stressed, they would approach the information desk with its large road map of the park under glass. Some would point to it and ask the question about where they were and where they were going wanting the ranger to show them their present location on the map and then point out how much farther they had to go to their destination, either Estes Park or Grand Lake. I think they just wanted some reassurance that they were on the right route.

– – – – – –

The national park was geographically divided into districts, including Thompson River, Wild Basin, and North Fork. Each had a district ranger and staff to serve visitor needs and respond to emergencies. Kurt Oliver and Bob Love were two of our highly skilled district rangers dedicated to serving the NPS mission and park visitors. The popular Wild Basin area in the southeast corner of the park included Ouzel Falls, Calypso Cascades, Thunder Lake, and many other great hiking destinations. There was a ranger office and trailhead parking just inside the entrance at Wild Basin.

One day three young college women, probably from the University of Colorado in Boulder, came into the main visitor center near Estes Park and asked at the desk, "How do we get to the 'WILD RANGER' Station?" Not knowing whether they were looking for a party or a hike, the person at the desk politely gave directions to the Wild BASIN Ranger Station and laughed to himself as the women left. They likely didn't find any wild rangers but they might have found Ranger Love.

Some of my other favorite questions asked of our staff included:

Is the altitude the same in the summer as it is in the winter? (It's hard to know how to answer this one other than yes.)

What is the best way to get to the backcountry campsites? (Walk)

When do the deer turn into elk? (Some locals like to say September 15 and hope they come back.)

Wow, those animals are neat; are they reindeer or caribou? (Elk)

Is the water cold in Iceberg Lake? (Duh)

Where is the Continental Divide? We just drove over Trail Ridge Road from Grand Lake to Estes Park and we didn't see it. (You drove over it – there is no bump or crest in the road.)

To an attractive ranger: I have two questions: Is Longs Peak open and are you busy tonight?

Can I wear deodorant in the backcountry, or will I be attacked by bears? (They might be attracted to stinky people.)

Is the Pool deep enough for a diving board? (The Pool is a natural deep spot on the Upper Thompson River along a popular hiking trail, not a good place to swim with or without the diving board.)

If I hike to the end of a trail, can my wife bring the car to pick me up? (Sorry motor vehicles, helicopters and drones are prohibited.)

During a particularly dry period, a ranger told the group: "Absolutely no fires are permitted!" One person asked, "How about campfires?"

Flattop Mountain has been called Flat Iron Mountain and Flat Tire Mountain.

A visitor said to a ranger on their day off, who was in uniform the day before: "You look different with clothes on"

Can I carry my ice chest to the Three Mile Campsite? (If you want to.)

Sorry, I can't hear you with my sunglasses on. (You are inside anyway, so it is better to take them off.)

I saw two tents at a backcountry campsite; are tents furnished for all backcountry sites? (No, the campsite happened to be occupied.)

If there is snow, will it be cold?

If I fall from Longs Peak, how far will I fall? (It depends, but a long way!)

Is the road to Longs Peak open? (No road, it is an eight-mile hike.)

– – – – – –

We also received interesting letters, prior to email of course, like my favorite one below:

Dear Ranger:

My name is Howard Yoon. I am 12 years old and I want to be a park ranger. I am coming to Rocky Mountain National Park this summer. Please look for me. You will recognize me by my Korean dad, my short mom, and my annoying sister. Your friend, Howard

– – – – – –

My broad responsibility as Rocky's chief of operations was incredibly interesting, and I thoroughly enjoyed being closely involved with all aspects of field operations. After seven years of working six or seven days per week from May through October, I was ready for a new assignment. Coincidentally, a friend of mine who was superintendent of Black Canyon of the Gunnison National Monument told me he was also looking for a new challenge. As it turned out, we decided to trade positions if we could obtain the necessary approvals from the regional director. Soon after, my family and I were moving to Gunnison, Colorado. The town is on the Western Slope and in a basin surrounded by mountains, with the well-deserved reputation as one of the coldest places in the U.S.

– – – – – –

CHAPTER SIX

BLACK CANYON OF THE GUNNISON NATIONAL MONUMENT AND CURECANTI NATIONAL RECREATION AREA, COLORADO

Superintendent 1996-2003

Befose Black Canyon became a national park, some visitors would drive the scenic South Rim Drive, stopping at the many canyon overlooks, and return to the visitor center to inquire, "The canyon is beautiful, but where is the monument? We couldn't find the monument." The title "national monument" was misunderstood by some, as they searched fruitlessly for a stone obelisk or brass plaque of some kind.

The 2,250 feet high Painted Wall with pegmatite dikes – the squiggly lines.

In 1906, Congress passed and President Theodore Roosevelt signed into law the Antiquities Act, giving the president the authority to establish by proclamation national monuments from federal lands to protect significant natural, cultural, or scientific features. Black Canyon of the Gunnison was designated a National Monument by President Herbert Hoover in 1833. All other units of the National Park System (national parks, national historic sites, national recreation areas, and more) require an act of Congress to establish. Many national parks were set aside and protected first as national monuments, such as Acadia, Zion, Grand Canyon, Bryce, Olympic, Arches, and Glacier Bay. As of early 2020, there are 419 units of the National Park System, including sixty-one with the national park designation.

– – – – – –

Even though Black Canyon of the Gunnison National Monument was already protected as a unit of the National Park System and managed by the National Park Service, it was a big deal when Congress passed legislation to change the designation to a national park late in 1999. Worldwide some thirty-eight newspapers carried stories about Black Canyon as a "new national park in Colorado." Locally, there was also great media interest in the new national park. I took many phone calls from news outlets and did several TV interviews. During one interview, a Denver reporter was taping our conversation at an overlook across from the Painted Wall, one of the most dramatic features of the park. It is a sheer vertical face 2,250 feet, making it the tallest cliff face in Colorado. The lighter color squiggly lines throughout the wall's surface are pegmatite dikes crosscutting through the older gneiss and schist. The reporter asked, "What is the primary rock seen here?" and pointed to the canyon and the Painted Wall. I said, "Schist," and he quickly replied, "Oh no, we can't say that word on TV! Can you call it something else?" That question and answer were edited out for the TV story that aired the next day. Changing the designation to Black Canyon of the Gunnison National Park was not an easy thing to accomplish. It required an act of Congress, passed by both the Senate and the House of Representatives and signed by the president. In fact, there had been several failed attempts before my arrival as superintendent.

— — — — — —

Top: One of the South Rim overlooks at Black
Canyon of the Gunnison National Park.
Bottom: Glimpses of the Gunnison River over 2,000 feet below.

For economic reasons, many in the Montrose business community wanted to have Congress change the name. Because most tourists have no doubt about the scenic grandeur of a national park, that title can be a much stronger attraction than the confusing title of national monument. The Montrose Chamber of Commerce was the primary proponent of the legislation due to the potential for boosting the local economy through increased tourism. The probabilities were high that there would be another attempt to pass legislation during my tenure, and I wanted to be ready with a new proposal that would provide greater benefit to Black Canyon.

- - - - - -

When I came to Black Canyon in 1996, the most visited part of the park was South Rim Drive. The North Rim was more remote and had fewer visitor facilities. The first time I drove the park road on the South Rim, I was surprised to encounter a few cows along the road. I soon learned that there was extensive private ranchland along the South Rim Drive owned by the Sanburg family. Ranchland in Colorado, especially in scenic areas, was under tremendous pressure because of increasing land prices and subdivision. It was not uncommon for rising land prices to tempt ranchers to sell off all or parts of their land as the economics of ranching became more challenging. It was obvious to me that this large area of private property (over 2,000 acres) could be split up as one or more residential subdivisions. House lots in scenic areas sell quickly and bring private roads, streetlights, noise, and houses, along with other incompatible uses that would diminish the existing wilderness character of the park.

- - - - - -

During previous attempts at a name change, the Department of the Interior did not support a change in designation primarily because the two bureaus that managed the land (the National Park Service and the Bureau of Land Management) did not agree on the approach. A formal study done by the NPS had concluded that the best way to make Black Canyon a national park would be to add more land along the river, specifically 50,000 acres of BLM-protected land called the Gunnison Gorge. No land management agency wants to give up some of its most spectacular land even to a "sister" bureau. There was also a sense of competition since the NPS typically received more public recognition and support, which often translated to more funding from Congress. It was highly unlikely that BLM's position would change, so I decided to take a fresh look and possibly develop a different approach. Besides, I believed that the 50,000 acres in the Gunnison Gorge were already protected against potential future threats, and therefore, it was appropriate that existing BLM management should continue.

– – – – – –

One of Colorado's senators, Ben Nighthorse Campbell, had just been named chairman of the Senate Subcommittee on National Parks. Senator Campbell was more aware and supportive of local Colorado wishes and politics, so I assumed that he would soon reintroduce legislation to change the name. Furthermore, as subcommittee chair he was in an excellent position to assure progress on any new legislation, at least in the Senate.

While thinking about a new approach, I remembered the cattle on the park road and the potential for highly visible, incompatible development on the private land if ranching ended on all or part of those 2,000 acres. I began visiting Mrs. Sanburg (who owned the ranch) and her son Kurt, who was managing it, to learn more about their circumstances and interests. Kurt loved ranching and managing the land, but typical economic pressures always introduced uncertainty regarding the future of the family's ranch property.

Working with the Sanburgs and a private conservation group, The Conservation Fund, I proposed creating a conservation easement to protect their ranch within the park boundary. The Sanburgs would be paid for the conservation easement but would retain title to the property. The language in the easement would be negotiated, but one important goal would be to limit any future development on the ranch to areas where such building would not be within sight of park visitors. In return, the Sanburgs would be paid a lump sum of money

146

as determined by appraisals that considered the value of the property before and after the restrictions. Having the conservation easement on the 2,000-acre ranch would significantly improve the long-term protection of the spectacular canyon and ensure a high-quality visitor experience along the South Rim, the most visited part of the park. This was a true win-win situation for all parties. The Conservation Fund would purchase the 2,000-acre conservation easement from the Sanburgs and then hold that until the ranch could be added within the park boundary through the legislative process. Ultimately, NPS would acquire the easement from The Conservation Fund and work with the Sanburgs to build cooperation regarding its long-term protection. In addition, the Sanburg property had blocked public access to the extraordinary Red Rock Canyon area of Black Canyon — one of the prettiest and easiest routes to the river. Limited public access was negotiated as part of the easement deal.

No proposed legislation would succeed unless both the NPS and BLM agreed. Therefore, I worked with Allan Belt, BLM's area manager, to reach a compromise whereby the bureau would allow about 7,000 acres of its land, rather than the 50,000 acres in previous proposals, to be added to the NPS unit. One argument against previous proposals was that the national monument was too small to be a national park without significant additions. Including the Sanburg Ranch easement, this new concept would add more than 9,000 acres, which meant that the total acreage would compare favorably in size to Bryce Canyon, Acadia, and Virgin Islands national parks. From my perspective, the best part of this new approach was that the natural resources of the spectacular canyon and environs would be much better protected for present and future generations. Somehow, the previous unsuccessful proposals had overlooked the critical importance of maintaining the Sanburg Ranch as open and unde-veloped land along South Rim Drive.

In the end, the combination of Senator Campbell's key subcommittee chairmanship, community support, landowner agreement, Department of the Interior support, and most importantly, this creative new concept resulted in successful legislation establishing Black Canyon of the Gunnison National Park in October 1999.

– – – – – –

I was sitting at a picnic table overlooking the Black Canyon with James Doyle, one of Senator Campbell's legislative assistants, when he received a phone call that told him the legislation unanimously passed the Senate. We exchanged high fives and smiles since we both had worked hard for that moment. The House passed an identical bill by unanimous consent a few weeks later. It was the culmination of some fresh thinking and a great deal of work to get agreement from all the parties involved. It was also a victory for achieving the mission of national parks — better protection for the resources while providing for improved visitor enjoyment.

In October 1999, Senator Campbell invited me to come to Washington and attend the signing ceremony with President Clinton in the Oval Office. The phone call came just two days before the ceremony, and I needed to hurry to get to Washington from Gunnison, Colorado, a small town with infrequent air service. For the White House ceremony, I would need my dress uniform, but it was at the dry cleaner, which was closed for the day. One great thing about living in small towns is that it was easy to learn who the owner was and how to contact her. A few phone calls later, I spoke with her, and she said she would meet me at the store that evening to give me my uniform. My 6 a.m. flight through Denver and on to Washington took me the rest of the next day, and I arrived at a hotel late that evening.

The next morning, we met at Senator Campbell's office, and his staff drove us to the White House. Representative Mark Udall, Representative Scott McInnis, Senator Campbell's wife, Linda, two of the senator's key subcommittee staff, and I made up the official party. We arrived in two cars at the White House gate back when Pennsylvania Avenue was open to traffic. The senator identified himself, and I was surprised that the Secret Service did not verify who else was in the two cars. As required, we had submitted our full names, birthdates, and social security numbers ahead of time for background checks. Despite that, I was amazed at the ease with which we entered the South Portico and parked right in front of the West Wing executive offices, where a Marine in dress uniform opened the door as we approached.

While we were waiting in the reception area outside the Oval Office, the president's chief of staff, John Podesta, came out to brief us on what to expect after we entered the Oval Office. He said the president would see us for about fifteen minutes: there would be brief "chit-chat," followed by the formal signing, a photo op with the news media, and Q&A outside.

President Clinton was warm and charming. He seemed to be oblivious to any schedule, spending more than the allotted fifteen minutes with us. Many photos were taken. After the signing, he gave each of us one of the official pens used for the purpose. I found it curious that the president would use multiple pens to complete his signature, but of course that provided more official pens for gifts. When I returned to the park, I had the pen placed in the park's collection of historic objects since it was one of the most important days in the history of Black Canyon of the Gunnison National Park.

President Clinton, Senator Campbell, Congressman
Udall, Superintendent Steele, and Congressman
McInnis after the President signed the legislation designating
Black Canyon a National Park in 1999.

– – – – – –

The other big challenge at Black Canyon was the horribly inadequate and
outdated visitor center, which was in a doublewide trailer sitting on the South
Rim. It was provided to the park more than thirty-five years earlier as a temporary visitor information center. Over the years, the condition deteriorated, and
numerous attempts to get funding for a new building failed. Estimated costs
to build a new visitor center ranged from $3 million to $5 million, but new
visitor centers were out of favor with congressional appropriators, making the
prospects for government funding nearly impossible.

We decided we could no longer wait for Congress to allocate money for a
new structure, so I began looking for creative funding alternatives. I called Tim
Priehs, the executive director of the park's nonprofit partner, Southwest Parks

and Monuments Association (now the Western National Parks Association). It sells books and maps in many parks in the western half of the U.S. Tim told me that about $75,000 in the Black Canyon donation account could be used for a new visitor center. It was a good start. I then called the National Park Foundation, the official charitable partner of the NPS chartered by Congress to assist with funding for special projects, and I convinced them to match that money. Combining these funds, we were able to buy a custom log building from a local manufacturer, Frontier Log Homes, at a significant discount, which was the equivalent of another donation.

The new one-story building would fit the rim location nicely, although it would have twice the floor space of the doublewide trailer. It would have a small room, about the size of a double garage, with forty-four seats for showing the park's orientation video. The main room would have plenty of space for new educational exhibits on the canyon. With careful planning, using park work crews to do a large portion of the site preparation and the finish work, and complete the interior furnishings, we built the new visitor center for less than $500,000. This did not include the salaries of our own workers.

Our first goal was to use the already disturbed site of the doublewide trailer rather than damaging another location. The existing parking lot and small restroom building at the present site would save money. A second goal was to minimize disruption to visitors wanting information during construction, so we decided to close the old building at the end of September and try to open the new one early in the following season.

We sold the doublewide for next to nothing, but the advantage was that someone else would pay to remove it from the park at the end of September 1997. The day after the two old pieces were trucked away, our crew went to work to prepare the site, pour a foundation, and lay utilities before winter arrived. The log home company began building the structure on their property with the plan to number each piece, disassemble it, and then reassemble it on our foundation yet that fall. The delivered structure would have no roof, insulation, windows, or doors. Park crews would order materials and finish that work before it opened to the public.

The log truck arrived early one cold November morning. A crane lifted the logs into place in numbered order, and crews fastened each log to the one below. By the end of the day, the new walls and roof trusses were in place and ready for our crew to take over. The highest priority was to get the roof on to avoid the need to shovel out the building each time it snowed, although that happened twice before the roof was completed. We installed windows and doors, finished the electric service, and completed the inside finish work including carpeting. We also planned new exhibits that would be fabricated and installed before the first season ended. Our maintenance crew completed the construction while our education division developed the new exhibits.

Old doublewide modular visitor center is hauled away
to make room for the new log visitor center.

The process was not without challenges. When the building warmed up, we were shocked to find beetles coming out of the logs by the hundreds for a few days. These logs came from area pine trees that were likely killed by pine bark beetles that had nested in the trees. Warmer temperatures typically encouraged the spread of the unwanted pests. Fortunately, the predominant vegetation around the building was scrub oak, which was not attractive to the pine bark beetle. Once we disposed of the new crop of beetles, the problem was solved.

In the end, we had an attractive new visitor center with a large porch along one side and a deck on the back with lovely views of the canyon and respite from the hot summer sun. There was also a popular overlook just below the visitor center with a short trail leading to it. In late May 1998, the local high school band played at a dedication event. Senator Campbell, Congressman McInnis, and I spoke at the ceremony. Borrowing a phrase from my teenage daughter, I said the new visitor center was "way cool." The crowd of locals and visitors reacted positively to the new building. By taking the lead to replace the old trailer, we saved the government money and significantly improved the visitor experience much sooner than had we waited for a congressional appropriation.

We were so pleased with the appearance of the new building; we built a new entrance station and restrooms to match the log design. We also built a new entrance sign complete with the winning logo from a design contest held in the community. The newly named national park was going to attract more visitors, and we were now ready to serve them with appropriate new facilities.

Photo previous page: New log building assembled on the South
Rim. Photo this page: Old visitor center was removed in September
and the new visitor center was opened the following May.

– – – – – –

The national park itself contains twelve miles of the deepest and most
dramatic section of the Gunnison River canyon, but the canyon continues upstream into Curecanti National Recreation Area (an NPS site) and
downstream into Gunnison Gorge National Conservation Area (a BLM site).
Together the three protected areas encompass forty-eight scenic miles of the
Gunnison River, which flows into the Colorado River near Grand Junction,
Colorado, at the end of its 164-mile journey.

The canyon has challenged explorers, both historically and today. In 1853,
the U.S. Army sent John Gunnison into the area looking for a railroad route.
He reported back that this portion of the river gorge was "impassable." In
1883, the Denver and Rio Grande Railroad hired Byron Bryant to survey the
canyon, looking for a possible rail alignment. Expected to be a twenty-day trip
with twelve men, their exploration lasted sixty-eight days, and only five men
completed the journey. It is easy to see why.

More recently, the huge rocks strewn about the bottom of the canyon, the many steep drops, the rugged character of the canyon, and difficult access to the water prevent almost all attempts to run the river either in a kayak or a raft. One expert kayaker died attempting to go over a waterfall during my tenure. Also, a fisherman died trying to cross the rushing river. His body was never found, likely because he was swept under house-sized boulders where the river completely disappears from view. A group of Navy Seals came to help, but after surveying the situation they agreed that it was too dangerous to swim under the rocks.

The canyon's name derives from the fact that parts of the gorge only receive thirty-three minutes of direct sunlight a day, according to *Images of America: The Black Canyon of the Gunnison*. Author Duane Vandenbusche states, "Several canyons of the American West are longer, and some are deeper, but none combines the depth, sheerness, narrowness, darkness, and dread of the Black Canyon. The Gunnison River drops an average of thirty-four feet per mile through the entire canyon, making it the fifth steepest mountain river descent in North America. The greatest descent of the Gunnison River occurs within the park at Chasm View, dropping 240 feet per mile. At its narrowest point the canyon is only forty feet wide at the river." The deepest part of the canyon is at Warner Point on the South Rim, where it is over 2,720 feet to the river below. The average water temperature is fifty degrees.

- - - - - -

As with my experiences in other parks, being a superintendent at Black Canyon was a great job — but not without its challenges. During my tenure, I was part of an official group that held a public meeting to discuss Black Canyon's federal reserved water right. Water rights are both extremely important and highly emotional issues in Colorado where not everyone can get all the water they need each year. The saying, "first in time, first in line," means the older dated rights receive priority even in the driest years. The senior water right holders get all of the water they need before those with junior rights get any, according to Colorado water law. The public meeting was called by the National Park Service to announce that we intended to exercise our 1933 water right for 300 cubic feet per second of flow to preserve the role of water in the canyon. Many people or ranches with junior water rights (later than 1933) could be affected by our use, and most of them were at this meeting to argue their cases. While I was answering questions, from the back of the room came "get a rope" and a little later, "Where is Timothy McVeigh when we need him?" (McVeigh was the bomber of the Oklahoma City federal building in 1995.) Fortunately, mob mentality did not take over, and the meeting broke up with no other threats. However, I wondered if I might encounter additional animosity at home or work.

– – – – – –

As superintendent of Black Canyon, I was also the superintendent of Curecanti National Recreation Area. The same management staff served both parks from the headquarters complex fifteen miles west of Gunnison, Colorado. Curecanti is a series of three reservoirs: Blue Mesa, Crystal, and Morrow Point. Blue Mesa is the largest body of water in Colorado and easiest to access as you drive along U.S. Highway 50 between Gunnison and Montrose. With two full-service marinas in the recreation area, boating and fishing are the most popular activities, although visitors also come to camp and hike. Hunting is also popular on other public land that surrounded these two parks. The National Park Service offers a scenic cruise on Morrow Point Reservoir. The 90-minute ranger guided tour cruises along the bottom of a deep canyon, with the tour boat dock about a three-quarter mile walk from the trailhead and parking area. Many people enjoy the leisurely boat cruise on the reservoir. Morrow Point is located deep in a spectacular granite canyon with such features as the Curecanti Needle, a dramatic spire, and nearby Chipeta Falls.

Chipeta Falls as seen from the tour boat on Morrow Point Reservoir.

- - - - - -

One day I received a phone call from a representative of a well-known teenager with a famous family name who wanted to charter the tour boat on Morrow Point Reservoir for a birthday party. They wanted the pontoon boat for two to three hours, which is about twice as long as the regular boat tour. Once they had reserved the boat for their specified date and time, the representative asked if there was a way to get the party supplies and food to the boat without walking the three-quarters of a mile path, which includes about 200 wooden steps. We said unfortunately not; that is the only way. Then the representative said, "Well, that's going to be a problem, especially for the kegs of beer." At this point, the conversation turned more serious. We should have been more suspicious from the beginning, since this particular individual was rumored to indulge in underage drinking. Ultimately, they had to find another venue for the beer party. In situations like these, I always thought of the potential negative headlines from a serious incident of any kind, and I didn't want something to reflect poorly on NPS.

Welcome to cowboy country — real cowboy country where young men wear their slickers, boots, and cowboy hats to school every day. And they tend to cattle after school and on weekends.

Not long after taking the job as superintendent of these two parks, I was driving the forty-five minutes between park headquarters and Black Canyon on U.S. Highway 50 when I came upon a pickup truck on the side of the road with a crudely hand-lettered sign that said "slow." As I was thinking about the meaning of that sign, I rounded the corner to find hundreds of cattle slowly walking down the highway with a few cowboys on horseback pushing them along. They were moving the cows from one pasture to another, a fairly common practice but not typically on a major US highway. I slowed to a crawl, and one of the cowboys motioned me forward until I was a few feet from the cows in the back of the herd. With his encouragement to keep moving, I inched forward until the cows divided. As I kept going, they soon surrounded my car, and all I could see were the butts of several hundred cows. As I continued to drive forward slowly, they moved from the front of my car to the sides and then the back until I came out the other side of the herd. That appeared to be standard practice in this important ranching area.

A few months later, in late November, I was driving south to the San Luis Valley on curvy Colorado Route 14 with my family. We were headed to a small town to help distribute toys at a charity event organized by a Gunnison church. The route took us through a fairly steep walled canyon. Given that the air temperature was in the high teens, black ice was a particular threat on the areas of highway still in shadow. Once I came out of one darker section of road into the sun and a drier highway surface, I increased my speed to avoid arriving late. The canyon turned again and as I rounded the corner, just in front of me was a group of cowboys on horseback moving cattle down the road. I slammed on my brakes only to continue to slide toward the men and cows on more ice. Fearing I was not going to stop before hitting a horse or the cows barely twenty feet in front of my car, I laid on my horn. In unison the cowboys turned and gave me what I would call nasty looks, as if I were trespassing on their turf. Fortunately, the combination of madly pumping my brakes and having the cowboys move to one side avoided a serious accident. I slid to a stop a few feet from the first cow. With horses standing tall, a vehicle that hits a horse (or moose) can result in front seat fatalities as the animal crashes through the windshield.

— — — — — —

When our kids were still pretty young, we took a nice four-mile hike from Pioneer Point Lookout down to the bottom of the canyon below and out to the end of the trail at the edge of Crystal Reservoir. It was easy going down a number of switchbacks and along a pretty cascading creek. A dense band of willow bushes lined one side of the creek, and the trail was on the opposite side. Pioneer Point Lookout was directly above the end of the trail at the reservoir, some 1,000 feet difference in elevation.

As we arrived at the edge of the reservoir, we heard yelling from above. We looked up, seeing maybe a dozen people yelling and waving at us from the lookout above. We waved back. An hour or more later, when we finished climbing the switchbacks to get back to the trailhead, a gentleman was aiming a video camera at us. He said, "Didn't you hear us yelling at you?" We said we did and that we waved back to what we thought was just a friendly group. He went on to say, "There was a bear following you all along the creek part of the trail. The bear was on the other side of the willows and just behind you as you hiked." We went over to the lookout and peered down into the canyon. Sure enough, we saw a black bear working his way along the creek. The man offered to show us video of the bear following us, so we went back to his RV at the campground to watch it. We were glad that we were unaware of the bear at the time since our kids were often ahead of us on the trail. Fortunately, black bears are normally not aggressive or threatening.

– – – – – –

The park ranger called dispatch to say the engine in his cruiser was dead and wouldn't start. We sent someone to pick him up and a wrecker to get the vehicle. When asked what might be wrong with the car, the ranger reluctantly told us the full story. As he was driving down the highway, his right hand was resting on the shotgun mounted between the two front seats parallel to floor. The safety on the shotgun was not on as it should have been, and the ranger accidentally fired the weapon. The deer slug went through the floorboard and into the engine block, and he coasted to the road shoulder as the engine died. He became known as "the ranger that killed his vehicle." He was a seasonal ranger, and he figured there was no need to apply for that job again next year.

While the previous story might suggest otherwise, rangers are well trained. Once I was out in a boat with our district ranger and a television news crew doing a general story on Curecanti National Recreation Area. The ranger was performing routine boat checks along the way, which entailed pulling along-side another boat, and checking for life vests and other required safety equipment. As we approached a boat with a family with four children aboard, the camera person asked our ranger to have his gun out of the holster as if we were approaching some "bad guys." The ranger politely declined, and I explained that it was not only contrary to common sense but also would have probably scared the family without good reason.

When I first joined the National Park Service, most park rangers were what we called "generalist rangers" who did everything from wildlife management to minor maintenance, education, search and rescue, and law enforcement. They rarely carried a gun, although they had a weapon in their briefcase or patrol vehicle. That slowly changed over the first half of my career, and now law enforcement rangers are highly specialized and well trained. They have to pass a battery of tests after attending the Federal Law Enforcement Academy, and they must take 40 hours of refresher training annually. Being in the field of law enforcement is more serious today. These rangers always have their gun and equipment belt on and are required to wear body armor under their shirts.

With more people carrying personal weapons, today's rangers must be prepared to deal with unexpected threats.

Today's generalist rangers are those who work in visitor services at the visitor centers or campgrounds or present public programs. They are not involved in law enforcement, but they are involved in all other ranger duties, including search and rescue, emergency medical services, wildland firefighting, visitor education and orientation, and off-site programs. To the public, everyone in the National Park Service uniform is a "ranger."

– – – – – –

In 2002, I applied for and was accepted into Senior Executive Service training, which would qualify me to manage the largest national parks in the system, including Yellowstone, Yosemite, Grand Canyon, and other sites of similar complexity and scale. During that one-year program, I applied for the superintendent's position at Acadia and was selected in early 2003. Barb and I moved there in May of 2003 after completing the SES program. I found Acadia to be an ideal situation with challenging issues, strong community support, and great partners, volunteers, and donors eager to help. It was such a good fit for my skills and interests, I decided there was no need to apply for any of those larger parks.

CHAPTER SEVEN

ACADIA NATIONAL PARK, MAINE

Superintendent, 2003-2015

Acadia National Park is the crown jewel of the North Atlantic Coast. It protects the natural beauty of the highest peaks on the Eastern Seaboard, rugged pink granite headlands along the Atlantic coastline, an abundance of wildlife habitats, and significant biodiversity. It has clear inland ponds and streams, dark night skies, and a rich history of individual actions to acquire the land and develop this popular national park in Maine for the benefit of all Americans. Historic resources include the forty-five miles of carriage roads with sixteen cut stone bridges, used today primarily for bicycling, and 130 miles of beautiful hiking trails, several with iron rung ladders to climb. Well-known landmarks that define Acadia's coast include the Bass Harbor Head Lighthouse, Thunder Hole, Great Head, Sand Beach, Otter Cliffs, Cadillac Mountain, and six other peaks above 1,000 feet. Barb and I smiled at the thought of peaks over 1,000 feet since we had moved from Colorado where numerous peaks were over 12,000 feet. In addition, Acadia includes Schoodic Point and numerous islands to explore, with interesting names like Great Cranberry, the Porcupines, Rum Key, and Little Moose. Acadia National Park is a paradise for hikers, kayakers, sailors, bikers, sightseers, photographers, and history buffs. It's no wonder that Acadia receives more than three million visits per year, including 180 cruise ships that stop in Bar Harbor annually.

Top: Popular Sand Beach in Acadia National Park. Bottom: Early morning at Monument Cove along Acadia's rugged granite coast.

Paddling up Northeast Creek in the fall to collect wild cranberries.

— — — — — —

During our first weekend at Acadia and on a seemingly rare dry day, my wife and I decided to take a bike ride on the carriage roads and experience the park as many visitors do. Several bikes were available to employees on a loan basis at park headquarters. Ranger Kevin Langley showed us where the bikes and helmets were kept and watched as my wife took a trial ride around the parking lot. Neither of us had ridden a bike in many years, so it is no wonder she was quite wobbly to start. Kevin watched her and then looked at me and touched the park radio on his belt as he said with a smile, "I'll keep my radio on." Thankfully, old skills returned and it was an uneventful ride. It was great to see the many families out enjoying *their* national park. I always try to remind folks that the national parks belong to all Americans, and we park rangers are just the caretakers.

We had arrived just before Memorial Day weekend in 2003 and temporarily moved into the old superintendent's house that was now used for seasonal employee housing. With two to a bedroom, the house could hold ten seasonal employees. It was important for the park to provide seasonal housing since available private rentals were not only scarce but expensive, much the same as in any major resort area. Local employers had the same issue of finding housing for employees, and many of them lived in substandard conditions, but were still glad to have the job. Acadia normally hires more than 150 seasonal employees who work from three to six months. Without government housing, many would not come, and others would not stay. Income from the monthly rent payments is put into a special account to help maintain park housing at an acceptable standard.

Having just moved from sunny Colorado to Acadia and Bar Harbor, we were soon wondering if we had done the right thing. We were welcomed by rain that continued for twenty-eight of thirty days during our first month. We scratched the sun porch idea from our house search, and we ordered waterproof L.L. Bean boots and rain pants in order to continue our daily walk routine.

We found a house to buy in Bar Harbor and moved in six weeks later. It is good for the park superintendent to live in the community. It improves community relations and helps the new superintendent make friends and develop new perspectives on the important relationship between the park and the surrounding towns. It used to be the tradition for the park superintendent to live in a specially designated house inside the park, but over time those houses were converted to other park uses such as office space or short-term housing. Acadia's former superintendent's house had five bedrooms, three bathrooms, and three fireplaces on a quiet lane called Old Farm Road.

Although we only lived in this house for a few weeks, we quickly learned we were not alone. Lying in bed, we heard critters in the walls, probably mice, and found a large black snake living in the basement. Sadly, we couldn't use the fireplaces because they were considered unsafe due to lack of maintenance over many years. Park budgets are always tight, and many maintenance needs were so far down on the list, some tasks were never completed.

Living in park housing had other disadvantages too. Despite the surrounding beauty, personal privacy can sometimes be sacrificed in the name of public service. I have known park employees who lived near a popular visitor facility such as a picnic area, and they often had people knocking on their door asking to borrow some catsup or lighter fluid or even a grill. Employees living in historic structures like Acadia's two uniquely designed gate houses on the carriage roads often had people looking in the windows or taking photos of the house from the yard. Even the "Private Residence" sign didn't discourage some nosy visitors.

One of two historic gate houses on the carriage
roads, used for summer employee housing.

- - - - - -

The superintendent of Acadia is another good example of being "a big fish in a small sea." Maine's total population is just over one million people and the largest city, Portland, is just over 100,000. Bar Harbor had some 5,000 year-round residents, but the entire island swells to over 40,000 when summer residents and hotels guests are counted. There is growing concern that Maine's total population is shrinking, with young people finding it particularly hard to find steady employment. Many Mainers have multiple part-time jobs and do different things in the winter than during the summer's boom.

Acadia is widely recognized as the state's number one tourist attraction, and it is the economic engine that generates millions of dollars in spending and produces thousands of jobs for the people of Maine. The national park receives a lot of attention and so does the superintendent. I was surprised when David Rockefeller Jr. held a reception for the new superintendent (me) at his summer house in Seal Harbor. Even Governor John Baldacci flew to Acadia by helicopter from the capital for the event. That would be unheard of in more heavily populated states.

It was the first of many cocktail parties where "casual dress" meant coat and tie. The social life for the park superintendent was busy, especially in July and August when longtime summer residents return. The summer community was made up of many prominent families who returned to Acadia each summer, sometimes for generations. Garden parties, day cruises on the water, cocktails, gala fundraisers, and going out to dinner with a growing number of friends became the routine. It is important for the superintendent to meet and establish close ties to many of the people who support the park as volunteers, donors, or board members of one of several nonprofit partners.

- - - - - -

We particularly enjoyed the real Maine accent, but it took some getting used to. True Mainers drop the "r" in most words. Bar Harbor becomes "Baa Haba" and my wife Barb became "Bob." The first time I answered our phone and the caller asked to speak to "Bob," I said, "Sorry, I think you have the wrong number." The caller said, "This isn't Bob Steele's number?" I thought to myself, Oh, you mean Barb. Another example would be "poc ya caa ova theya" or "park your car over there." I did laugh at the sign selling "fiyah" wood using the Maine accent as a marketing strategy. The seller also advertised it as "organic." Only people born in Maine are true Mainers, and everyone else is "from away."

Living on the coast, we assume that generally people "from away" know things that they don't. Tidal changes, especially the thirteen-foot large tides of Maine, are an example. Visitors new to Maine and to the coast have come to the park's information station or the Chamber of Commerce office and say, "Wow! You must be in a terrible drought; the water is sooo low!" when the mud flats are actually a result of low tide. Another question that "in-landers" sometimes ask, "How do they get all the boats to park facing one way?" When we explain that the anchors or moorings allow the boats to swing with the wind, they real-ize that all the boats are facing into the wind. Occasionally some wise guy will answer that question by simply saying, "It is a town ordinance."

Some of the many fishing boats in Bar Harbor with
the Porcupine Islands beyond the boats.

At the park, we strive to give respectful and informed answers. Our main visitor center at Hull's Cove was not designed for the crowds they now get. On a busy day, we could have more than 5,000 people through the relatively small building. On those peak summer days, there will be multiple lines of people waiting to see the rangers behind the visitor counter. If there are four uniformed rangers at the desk, there will be four lines of people patiently waiting their turn.

I have had an occasion to arrange to meet someone at the visitor center for a tour or other official activity, and while I waited (in uniform), a line of visitors would quickly form in front of me. When those people saw a ranger with no line, they thought it was their lucky day. I really enjoyed talking to visitors, but it is hard to break away when the time comes.

– – – – – –

As the new superintendent, one of my staff arranged an evening public meeting on Isle au Haut to introduce me to the community and to answer questions about a park planning effort related to the island, much of which is part of Acadia National Park. About two-thirds of the island is within the national park, and there are about seventy year-round residents. To get to the meeting would require a two-hour drive from park headquarters to Stonington, Maine, and then a boat trip of forty-five minutes to the isolated island. Ranger Charlie Jacobi made the arrangements, and I asked him for an early departure so I could tour the remote island. I also wanted to meet the small staff as part of my orientation to this mostly wilderness part of Acadia. We planned to take the 10:30 a.m. ferry, which would give us all afternoon to tour the island's park trails, small campground, and ranger office. Because I don't do well without regular meals and because the island has no restaurants, we decided to pick up lunch and dinner on our way to meet the boat. We left headquarters at about 7:30 to have plenty of time to make the food stop along the way. The first place we stopped did not start lunches until 10, and we could not wait. The second place did not open until 11. Charlie said not to worry; we would just go to the grocery store before we went to the ferry. With a few minutes to spare, we pulled up to the only grocery store in Stonington and were surprised to find a large "out of business" sign on the door. With little time left, we went straight to the dock with Charlie giving me assurance that a small store on Isle au Haut had food to buy. That store was only open a few days a week from 10 a.m. to 2 p.m., and fortunately, today was one of those. At the town dock we went straight to the store, and although options were limited, I bought both lunch and dinner. Because I knew I would be lucky to get home by midnight,

I bought a package of baloney (which I hadn't eaten in years), a loaf of bread, and a small package of cookies. At least this was something to keep my stomach from growling during the meeting. After lunch, I mentioned to the island ranger our problems getting lunch and dinner food. He said, "Oh, you are in luck. This is Thursday, and Betty, a local mother of two, makes and sells pizza from her garage." At 5:30 we went to her garage, chose the pizza toppings, and waited while it baked it in her outdoor oven. The pizzas were terrific, and they sure beat another baloney sandwich.

— — — — — —

The family was waiting anxiously as water rose around their car. Tide was coming in and the car could be submerged within the hour. Crossing the sand and rocky bar from Bar Harbor to Bar Island was a popular excursion, but people are warned to pay attention to the local tide chart. After all, the swing from low tide to high tide can be as much as twelve to thirteen feet, normally occurring twice a day. When the tide is coming in, the water level rises at about two feet per hour or two inches every five minutes. Today, the tow truck arrived in time for the operator to wade out, attach a cable to the car, and pull it to shore before water entered the passenger compartment. Many others haven't been as lucky.

Daily, several hundred people walk the one-third mile across the bar to Bar Island where they can hike to a popular viewpoint that looks back over to Bar Harbor and Mount Desert Island. Park rangers and locals warn people that they have about two hours on either side of low tide to make the crossing and return before the bar is covered again. Some people want to drive across to say they have driven to an island in Maine that does not have a bridge or ferry to it. They drove on the "ocean bottom" to get there. Occasionally people lose track of time or forget exactly when low tide is, and they end up stuck on the island.

171

Several hundred people a day walk across the bar to Bar
Island at low tide. The bar can be exposed or
under 6 feet of water, depending on the tides.

People planning on walking over and back are usually careful to avoid problems with timing. However, an often-asked question in town is the depth of the water across the bar at high tide. It's a logical question because people want to know if they do get stuck, can they wade back or will it be too deep? Some locals like to give the answer to the depth question this way: "It is about twelve inches from the top of a Cadillac Escalade," and yes, that has been proven. Even with all the warnings, an average of one vehicle per year needs to be towed off the bar. If it is too long before the tow truck gets there, the vehicle can be completely submerged, and a vacation ruined.

Those who get stuck on Bar Island by the rising tide have several choices. They can try wading back if the water is just beginning to cover the bar, they can yell for help and a boater might pick them up, or harbor master might come get them (sometimes for a fee), or they can wait six to eight hours for the next low tide window of opportunity. I have seen a number of people wading back, but the footing is tricky, the water cold (fifty-nine degrees at best), and it takes longer than one thinks when you can't see the rocky bottom. I watched as one couple began crossing in knee-deep water, and soon the man was far ahead of his wife or girlfriend. She turned back and he continued. Even if he sent a boat back for her, I am sure there was a heated discussion later that evening.

Just before I retired, I received an email from a woman who usually walks her dog across the bar and back anytime the tides allow her to do it in the early morning. On one particular morning, she and her dog arrived on the other side where the park has placed a critter proof trash can on the slope as you climb up onto the island. On this day, as she approached, she could see trash, including some clothing items scattered around. She immediately thought an animal had gotten into the trash can while looking for food and left a real mess. Being a good citizen, she decided to pick it up and place it back in the can.

She told her dog to sit, and began picking up the larger items when she heard from inside the can. "Hello?" Startled, she said hello back, and from inside came a voice, "I'm in here." Once the lid is closed, it requires someone on the outside to insert their hand to release the latch and open it, which she did. Inside was a teenage boy wrapped in the plastic trash bag but with no clothes on.

He explained he had come over to walk the island and did not check the tides or the time. When he went to return across the bar, water had already covered it. He tried to wade across, but he turned back and decided to wait for the next low tide. By that time, he was soaking wet and getting cold. He took the trash bag out of the can, dumped the trash and wrapped it around him. Then he decided to get out of the wet clothes. As night approached and he got colder, he decided to get into the trash container, inside the plastic bag, and wait for morning. The boy was embarrassed, but otherwise fine. The dog-walking woman is a reputable person and not prone to making things up, but this story illustrates that truth can be stranger than fiction.

- - - - - -

I liked to encourage our park management team (superintendent, deputy, and the division chiefs) to spend some time observing operations or visiting employees and volunteers on the job, whether it is at the visitor center, or along the road, or at a more remote project site. I would often wear my uniform on weekends and go on hikes, or stop at overlooks and viewpoints to encounter visitors who wanted to make a comment or ask a question. It was nice to hear compliments: "The park is so beautiful and clean," "You have a great job," "I am glad our tax dollars help pay for national parks," or "How does one get a job in a national park?" Of course, the most common questions are "Where is the nearest restroom?" and "How do I get to Thunder Hole?" When big waves were crashing in, Thunder Hole is indeed spectacular with spray often soaking the viewing area, including anyone standing too close. However, on most calm days the action could be disappointing, and some locals would refer to it as "gurgling gulch."

Uniformed employees, who were out and around the park daily no matter their job title or work responsibility, were trained to consider providing visitor information as part of their job. Priscilla worked at Acadia for over forty-five summers as a seasonal laborer, cleaning restrooms and picking up roadside litter. She encountered hundreds of visitors in any given week, many with questions. She always tried to answer their questions or help if she could. Almost every day I would hear Priscilla on the park radio seeking help for another visitor. Fortunately, I think most people working for the National Park Service say that "service" is part of the title for a reason.

— — — — — —

Acadia's visitor count has gone up nearly 60 percent since 2006, and the annual count is now over three million visits. This makes Acadia one of the top ten most visited national parks in the country. Acadia also happens to be one of the five smallest parks in area (about 36,000 acres). These two statistics lead me to say that Acadia is "the most visited national park per acre." Clearly, we are serving large numbers of visitors in a relatively small area. (In contrast, Yellowstone covers more than two million acres.) This leads to many potential problems, such as crowded facilities, lack of parking, occasional gridlock on top of Cadillac Mountain, frustrations over not being able to get a campsite or a reservation at Jordan Pond House, and more. I recall one beautiful fall day when there were three large cruise ships in the harbor, and sixteen big buses were competing for five bus spaces on top of Cadillac. They began discharging passengers in the travel lanes, and soon it was complete gridlock. No one was having a quality visitor experience. When the numbers at the top become a problem, rangers barricade the entrance to the Cadillac Summit road until the congestion at the top has resolved itself as people leave. It's unfortunate that some visitors may not get to see the spectacular view from the summit, but other factors prevent good views too, such as fog, heavy rain, or nightfall.

Sunrise as seen from the top of Cadillac has become quite a phenomenon. Guidebooks write about it, and many say it is the first place in the United States where one will see the sunrise. Maine is as far east and north as one can be in the Eastern time zone. Despite the fact that the sun rises around 4:30 a.m. in June, there could be a hundred or more cars without parking spots. Even though these people had to get up early, it is a wonderful experience to see the sun rise over the islands of Frenchman Bay and the mountains of Maine. The last time I was up there for sunrise, I heard great comments from kids who said, "That was so cool!" and "This was the best vacation ever!" It is rewarding to have people inspired by nature and *their* national parks.

- - - - - -

Most people do not realize when they stop in Acadia for popovers at Jordan Pond House or a carriage ride at Wildwood Stables, these popular attractions are operated as concessions under contract to the National Park Service. Contracts are rebid approximately every ten years, and annual performance ratings by park staff play a significant role in the contract bidding and award process. Park staff monitors these contracts to assure high quality services. In addition to formal annual evaluations, we do routine price comparisons with similar operations outside the park to keep things reasonable.

During the first few weeks on the job as the new superintendent, I would try to get around to see as much of the park and its operation as possible while I still had a fresh perspective. Back in 2003 when I moved to Acadia, my mother and brother came for a visit, and they wanted to go on a carriage ride. This had the double benefit for me of seeing this activity with that fresh perspective and observing a concession operator without them knowing who I was. In that way my experience would be closer to those of our everyday visitors.

Heidi was our driver, and there were about a dozen people on this carriage, which was being pulled by four big, strong horses. Heidi told many stories, most of which were not directly related to the park or the history of the carriage roads. It was disappointing given that the carriage road story is not only relevant, but interesting. Our two-hour ride covered just a few miles of the forty-five miles of carriage roads available for horse use inside Acadia, and we saw several of the beautiful cut stone bridges.

Another carriage ride leaves Wildwood Stables, a park concession operation.

At the end of our carriage ride, Heidi said, "Thanks for coming today. I hope we will be here next year, but it is doubtful." I raised my hand and asked why they would not be here next year. She replied that the park was trying to "get rid of them and carriage rides." I asked why that would be the case given that the carriage roads were built for the purpose, and they were really part of Acadia's history. Her only answer was that Bill (not his real name), the manager of the Wildwood Stable concession, had told her that. After others had left, I introduced myself and told her that the National Park Service was *not* interested in having the carriage rides stopped, and that it was an important part of park history.

The following week, I decided to confront Bill to correct the misinformation that Heidi and other drivers were giving. I told him that these false accusations and made-up stories had to stop. In addition, I said it would be best if his drivers provided more accurate information and accounts of the history of Mr. Rockefeller's roads. He said they would. I offered to have our education staff work with him on training his drivers, but he declined the offer. Several months later, after directing my concessions staff person to follow up with Bill and to monitor progress, it was apparent that things were not changing, and the carriage ride experience continued to be less than satisfactory from my perspective. I invited Bill to a lunch meeting and told him that things needed to change. I said we would give his drivers better information from which to draw stories that would be historically accurate and more relevant to Acadia. I hoped the drivers would use that information on tours.

Again, after several months, feedback was still negative. I called Bill and said I would like to meet with all his drivers at one time, and the date and time was fixed. Upon arrival at the Wildwood Stables, I was met by Bob who worked for Bill, and he was videotaping me as I got out of my car and walked to the stables. The camera was just a few feet from my face. I walked to the barn and talked to the fifteen or more assembled drivers and was videotaped the entire time. I told them the park had no intention of kicking them out, and that carriage rides were both in keeping with Acadia's history and appropriate as long as the visitor experience was a good one. I used the example of the park's recent $1 million dollars in improvements as proof we intended to continue the carriage rides. One particular driver told me that Bill had claimed that he had invested that $1 million, not the park. I answered questions and emphasized the park goal was to improve the visitor experience and to make the narrative both accurate and interesting. Bob followed me to the car with his camera running. Upon return-ing to my office, I called Bill and asked him for a copy of the videotape so that I had a record of what was said at our meeting. Of course, I never received it.

Bill continued to be a problem partner seemingly looking for ways to make trouble. He even filed a complaint with the Maine Department of Environmen-tal Protection, suggesting that the park maintenance area was polluting Eagle Lake about a quarter mile away. After a site visit, state investigators determined there was no threat to Eagle Lake. They did, however, find a single spot of oil leaked from a dump truck that needed to be removed – about two wheelbarrows full that were treated as hazardous waste and disposed of properly. It puzzled me why Bill would file such a false complaint against the park knowing that it would only further strain our relationship. But that was Bill.

- - - - - -

Not long after that, I was informed by the White House that Laura Bush and four of her best friends would likely be visiting Acadia. Laura and her group picked a different national park each year for a week of hiking and other outdoor activities. The advance man (an army officer assigned to the White House) called my office as a preliminary step to determine if the visit would be a good fit for Mrs. Bush and her friends. He asked me to describe the various things that she and her friends could do. Seeming satisfied with my ideas, he said he and the White House doctor would visit in a few days. The White House doctor was an Iraq war veteran and Navy Seal surgeon who could probably operate on someone in a swamp in some faraway place. He walked many park trails in order to recommend those most suited to the first lady and her friends. We kept secret the possible itinerary to assure her safety and avoid forcing them to change plans or go elsewhere.

One of the ideas discussed was a carriage ride, and the advance man said they would like to arrange such a ride. Knowing that Bill with his negative views of the National Park Service and the park could be a big problem, I told the advance team that I would personally make the arrangements. I wanted to be in control. After he left, I drove down to the Wildwood Stables and waited for Jack to return from a ride. After all, Jack was clearly the best driver and narrator among all the drivers. Without divulging secrets, I told him that VIPs were coming, and I wanted *him* to give them a carriage ride. I told him this had to remain strictly between us, and I needed his personal information for a background check. We told Bill that we needed a carriage set aside on the given date for a party of guests from Texas, and we wanted Jack as the driver. No problem.

The day of the event, the motorcade with Laura Bush showed up for the ride, and Bill "flipped out." Seeing Laura Bush was there, he said, "I am taking this ride," and pushed Jack aside. The Secret Service agent in charge stepped up and said, "I am sorry, sir, but Jack is taking this ride." Bill protested, but the Secret Service said, "You have not been cleared by security and you will *not* be taking the first lady." Bill was upset and threatened to cancel the ride, but he soon realized that he would look foolish if he did not allow Jack to go. It made my day.

Rangers and other park staff worked alongside the Secret Service to make Laura Bush's week in Acadia both safe and enjoyable. As the week ended, the White House liaison for the trip said Mrs. Bush wanted to recognize and thank the park staff for all of their help to make her visit go smoothly. She asked for staff and their spouses to gather so she could personally thank them. We decided on a cocktail party, and the most private location with minimal security concerns was my house in Bar Harbor.

Security arrangements were interesting. First, as indicated earlier, the event had to be kept secret. One agent came to our house the day before and did a walk-through. Then a couple of hours before the first lady was to arrive, an undercover agent in an older model pickup sat outside our house to observe the neighborhood and be sure no one was lurking. As the motorcade pulled up, he went on to the next location on her schedule (dinner) for this important counter surveillance role. While the first lady was inside our house at this cocktail party style event, agents were posted at each door.

Two groups of men with earpieces in black cars sat in the neighborhood. One of our neighbors told us later that she had seen the car nearest her house and went down to ask them what was happening. Of course, they said nothing, they were just tourists. Their short hair and earplugs seemed to indicate otherwise. Our neighbor knew something was up, but she did not know what. Later when she and my wife were talking, she learned that Laura Bush had been right next door. Mrs. Bush was charming and friendly and even posed for photos with anyone who wanted one. Of course, everyone did.

– – – – – –

More recently, the new operator of Wildwood Stables called park dispatch one day with an urgent plea for help. One of his horses had fallen through the floor of the barn and was now stuck. The floor of the main stables was reinforced to prevent such accidents, but this horse had broken the rope that held him in his stall. He then wandered to the feed room, for obvious reasons, and that floor was not as strong. The horse was chest deep in this jagged hole in the floor. Once a veterinarian arrived and gave the horse a tranquilizer, rangers and maintenance crews rigged a rope and pulley system attached to the building's strong roof beams. It took some time and the strength of twenty people to raise the 1,600-pound horse and free him from his predicament. Other than a few leg scratches the horse was not seriously injured. Of course, the hole in the floor had to be repaired and the floor reinforced. Ranger Richard Rechholtz told me this was the most difficult rescue he had worked on in his twenty years at Acadia.

The 1600-pound horse was not supposed to be in the
feed room where it fell through the floor.

— — — — —

Occasionally, we might have to respond to two or more incidents at the same time, requiring us to assign rangers to multiple incidents at once. Fortunately, we could call upon a local volunteer search and rescue organization that often trained alongside park rangers when we needed extra help. One day we had a report of a twelve-year-old boy falling from his bike on the carriage roads and sustaining numerous abrasions. Two rangers entered the carriage road system in their patrol vehicle looking to provide first aid and determine the seriousness of the boy's injuries.

Meanwhile, Emily, the new manager of Wildwood Stables, had been hired to give a woman a custom carriage ride. While driving the carriage to some of the most scenic spots, Emily noticed a runaway horse (no rider) coming toward her. As it got closer, she saw the horse was spurting blood from a serious leg

181

wound. Emily and the woman both got off their carriage and tried to stop the coming horse. Once they got the horse stopped, Emily took off her blouse and wrapped the wounded and badly bleeding leg. Soon the other woman also donated her blouse. Later the local vet gave them credit for saving the life of that horse by stemming the loss of blood.

At the same time the two rangers were looking for the injured boy, they began seeing blood on the carriage road. Not knowing of the injured horse, they assumed the boy must be bleeding badly, and they reported their concerns to park dispatch. As the rangers came around a bend in the carriage road, they encountered the two women without their blouses holding a single horse and a stopped carriage. After checking with Emily, the rangers reported this accident and suggested the stables be notified of the need to come and assist Emily. Another mile up the carriage road, the rangers found the injured boy and transported him and his bike to a waiting ambulance. Luckily, his injuries were not serious. It was also fortunate that the rider of the injured horse was not seriously hurt either. As we would often say in Acadia, "You can't make this stuff up."

— — — — — —

An exception to most national parks, Acadia allows dogs on all park trails, except the unique ladder trails (more about these later), as long as they are leashed. This occasionally leads to problems when people let their dogs off leash as soon as they are away from the trailhead or when the dog has trouble with summer heat or an occasional close encounter with park wildlife. Summer temperatures can reach into the nineties with high humidity adding to the stress for some dogs. I have seen dogs, especially those with dark fur, seeking patches of shade under trees and bushes as their owners try coaxing them to climb higher. Some owners don't realize that dogs can be candidates for heatstroke, and park rescuers sometimes are called to carry pets out on stretchers when they collapse.

I remember an incident where a black lab named Chester suffered the equivalent of heatstroke. Fearing their dog might die, the owners called 911 for help. Once the dog was carried by stretcher down the mountain and put into an air-conditioned car for the ride home, the dog seemed to revive. The incident made the local paper with a photo of the dog on the stretcher looking miserable. The owner sent rangers a photo of the dog a few days later, fully recuperated and wearing its new hiking boots.

According to another ranger report: "A pair of dogs that found out about porcupine quills the hard way illustrates one of the reasons why pets need to be kept on leash." According to the report, "A man from the Bahamas hiked to the top of Parkman Mountain with his two dogs. They had been kept on leash, he told rangers, but he released the leads while he picked blueberries at the summit."

"That is when the dogs discovered a nearby porcupine," Chief Ranger Stuart West said. "A dog named Franny ended up with its muzzle, tongue, and gums covered in quills, but was able to walk down the trail on her own. The other dog, Felix, had similar injuries, but also had quills in his paws and was unable to walk. Felix was carried off the mountain on a stretcher by park rangers." A local vet removed the quills and provided much needed relief for the dogs.

With porcupine quills in his face and paws, rangers had to rescue this dog by stretcher.

－ － － － － －

Ranger Richard Rechholtz told me of an interesting incident involving him. Occasionally someone would drive through the entrance station without paying. The ranger at the fee station radioed dispatch with a description of the vehicle and the license plate, but the vehicle eluded park staff. Later that day, a boy had fallen into the rocks near Thunder Hole and was injured but not seriously. Richard responded, and the boy was lifted back up to the road and taken by ambulance to the local hospital. Richard went to the hospital to get some more information from the father for his report. During that process, Richard realized that the father's car and plates matched the description of the person not paying the fee earlier that day. When asked if he paid the fee, the father admitted he drove through the gate without paying. Richard told him that the entrance fees were important to the park and supported operations such as the rescue of his son.

Richard often dealt with the media after a rescue, and he was good about working important safety messages and other key information into the media coverage. The local paper would always include those messages, lessons learned or other park information such as the importance of the entrance fee to help pay for essential ranger services. These real-life rescue stories were widely read, and this helped us educate the public on proper preparation, trail etiquette, and ways to deal with potential problems while enjoying the park.

－ － － － － －

Driving away from park headquarters one day, I saw a loon in need of rescue. It was awkwardly walking along Eagle Lake Road near a shallow beaver pond on the north side of the road. The loon appeared to be injured, so I quickly turned around and returned to headquarters barely a mile away. There I enlisted our bird expert, Ranger Laura Haller, to come with me to see if we could help the loon. We pulled our car over to the side, she got out and threw a light jacket over the bird to reduce its stress and prevent it from fleeing from our help. She picked up the captured bird, and we drove it a short distance to the Eagle Lake boat ramp. Laura carried the loon down the ramp until she could place it on water a few feet deep. The bird immediately paddled out into the lake and gathered enough speed to slowly take off. We smiled at each other, pleased that the loon seemed to be fine and we had likely saved it from being hit by a car.

Laura explained that the legs on a loon are far back on its body, which makes it a great diver and swimmer but awkward on land. She surmised that the loon had landed on the nearby beaver pond by mistake, and when it could not take off from that small, shallow body of water, it proceeded to walk probably to Eagle Lake. Loons are a magnificent water bird, and we were glad we could help this one return safely to its preferred environment.

— — — — — —

Another connection between the Bush family and Acadia were two visits by daughter Jenna. The first was when her boyfriend brought her camping at Blackwoods Campground in the national park. As the daughter of the sitting president, she had Secret Service protection, and agents camped and hiked along with her. During that trip, Jenna's boyfriend asked her to hike up Cadillac Mountain for sunrise. As the sun rose in the east, the boyfriend proposed to Jenna on Cadillac, and she said yes.

During her second trip, as a correspondent and co-host for NBC's Today Show, she told us the story of that hike. She was embarrassed by the fact that she had hurried up the mountain and hadn't even brushed her hair or her teeth. She had had no idea that he was going to propose.

For her second visit, now as Jenna Bush Hager, she was to do a live feed from the coast of Acadia for the Today Show. The production team came two days ahead to prepare the location and to take additional video that could supplement her on-air time. The production people had two large, black SUVs full of their equipment. Late morning the next day, Jenna arrived from the Portland airport via a black limousine, which made the group of cars look quite official. I escorted them around the park as they visited a couple of locations in preparation for the live broadcast the following day. By this time, we had a small

185

procession of vehicles with my park car, complete with antennas and logo, in the lead. Two black SUVs and the limo plus my lead vehicle made it look like an official motorcade – unusual on Mount Desert Island and inside Acadia.

One of the producers had called a deli in Southwest Harbor for carry-out sandwiches, which we needed to pick up on our way through town. It was a typical busy summer day with a college student "rent a cop" directing traffic at the only main intersection in this small town. I knew parking for our four vehicles, even for a few minutes, would be a problem given the crowds. I spotted a section of no parking signs and yellow curbing right at that intersection, so I pulled over and the other vehicles followed me to the curb. Quickly spotted by the traffic cop, he came over to tell me to move on. But I spoke first and said, "President Bush's daughter is in one of these cars, and we only need to be here a few minutes." His demeanor instantly changed, and he said, "No problem, sir. Stay right there, just give me a signal when you are ready, and I will take care of everything." He returned to the center of the intersection with renewed vigor and purpose. When we were ready to pull out, I gave him a wave. Now standing a little taller, he loudly blew his whistle for what seemed like an unusually long time, stopping traffic in all directions. He then gave me a military style hand maneuver to move out. I am sure it was the highlight of his summer.

The next morning Jenna did her live segments from the pink granite coastline at Monument Cove inside Acadia. While she was on camera, we had arranged for a four masted schooner with red sails, the *Margaret Todd*, to pass just off the coast as background for the scene to be broadcast nationwide. The captain of the *Margaret Todd* was happy to provide the colorful backdrop given the free national publicity. It was one of several pieces of national coverage that put Acadia in the news and likely contributed to the increasing numbers of visitors.

Another such piece of publicity was when Good Morning America's viewers named Acadia "America's Favorite Place" in 2014. The winning destination was announced with another live broadcast, this time with Ginger Zee paddling a canoe on Jordan Pond. Mount Desert Island and Acadia made several other lists, including "top ten island destinations in the U.S." However, the most publicity worldwide was when President Obama and the first family came to Acadia in 2010.

- - - - - -

Late one day as I was preparing to leave the office, my phone rang, and the caller said he was with the White House. This got my attention especially since it did not sound like a prank call. He introduced himself as the director of the White House Advance Office and said the president and first family were considering coming to Acadia for an outdoor recreation three-day weekend. He wanted to know what kind of things they could do, so I described the hiking, biking, boating, and other possibilities. Evidently, he thought those would appeal to the family and said he would come the next day for a quick tour.

When he arrived, he came with a representative of the first lady's office and a senior person with the Secret Service. We took a tour of the park, and I pointed out various options for the Obamas to enjoy. He asked for three recommendations for short hikes and three suggestions for bike rides. I offered my ideas complete with trail length and estimated times of the hikes or rides. As they departed, he said they would discuss these ideas with the president and get back to me. Two days later, he called again to say that a larger advance group would arrive the next day for a closer look and for planning the details of the visit. This certainly implied they were coming. Of course, secrecy was important, and we were told not to share information with anyone who did not need to know. Initially, the chief ranger, the deputy superintendent, and I worked directly on planning for what would be a large group with many logistical and transportation needs and layers of security.

The next day about twenty people came to park headquarters, and soon the local police chief and a supervisor from the Maine State Police also arrived for a briefing in the park conference room. Employees in the building were suddenly aware something big was happening, but they didn't know what. Speculation and rumors ensued.

The advance team, mostly Secret Service and White House press office folks, wanted to look at each of my recommendations, which meant we took bike rides on all three of the sections of carriage road I suggested. Next were hikes on three trails. They took notes and discussed potential security issues. One question that arose involved weight allowances on the carriage road bridges. The heavy armored presidential limo would follow the family as they rode bikes on the carriage roads. The highly secure vehicle would need to be close by in case it was needed in an emergency. Acadia's engineer calculated the weight of one of our dump trucks filled with gravel at about 50,000 pounds. This information satisfied the secret service since it indicated there would be no problem for the armored limousine to drive over the bridges.

From one of the three suggested bike routes (around Eagle Lake), a short trail to Connor's Nubble offers a great view of Eagle Lake and surrounding parkland. I thought this short walk and climb would be a bonus and add a nice memory for the family's visit. The last short section of that quarter-mile hike was a bit of a scramble up and through some rocks for about a hundred yards. Despite the spectacular view from the top, the agent in charge quickly said, "This one is out. If one of the family or the president were to twist an ankle, it would be an international incident."

As we hiked the short and flat (1.8-mile loop) Ship Harbor Trail with the team, we noticed a large dead tree leaning over the trail. The leader asked me if I could get it removed. "No problem," I said. I radioed Gary Stellpflug our trails foreman, and told him of the tree and asked if he could get it down and removed. He said a crew could remove it next week, so I asked a little more emphatically. Could he do it *today*? Without any more explanation, he said, "I will take care of it personally."

That trail turned out to be the one the Obamas walked from the trailhead to the rocky coastline for the wonderful salt air and great ocean views. A few people were enjoying the rocky coast where the trail ends when the first family arrived, but the Secret Service decided other visitors would not be a threat since they would not have known of the president's plans or schedule. The surprised hikers were allowed to remain at a safe distance as the family approached. Among those few people were Gary and his wife who "happened" to be walking that particular trail that day. No need to speculate how he figured the president might be in that area.

Early in the planning, we were told the president's visit was to be kept secret until announced by the White House. I was surprised when it showed up in the local paper a few days before he was to arrive. Preparations were in full swing, especially at the Holiday Inn Regency where the family would stay. Rooms were painted, bulletproof glass placed in the windows, and I heard an armor plate was placed under the bed to protect from a blast below. A friend of mine was asked to obtain and hang new works of art in the recently refurbished and newly named "Presidential Suite." The large entourage of Secret Service and other staff would completely fill the hotel rooms and there were others in nearby hotels.

The local phone company, FairPoint, had a bad reputation for service with many complaints seemingly going unanswered. Cellphone coverage on Mount Desert Island was poor at best. To everyone's surprise, a few days before the president was to arrive, as many as twenty FairPoint company trucks were working all over the island correcting problems. Some people were amazed to find four bars of service when they usually had one or two, if any. What would happen when the first family left?

As the park superintendent, I was to be the official greeter, along with my wife, Barb, on top of Cadillac Mountain, the first presidential stop in the park. The first family would take a short walk around the summit to enjoy the spectacular views of Frenchman Bay, the Porcupine Islands, and the surrounding mountains. The only problem was heavy fog that particular morning, but it was breaking up. As we waited, the Secret Service agent in charge, gave my wife a large lapel pin to wear that would indicate she had been cleared to be close to the president. Since I was in uniform and easily recognizable, I did not need a pin. Barb returned from a quick trip to the restroom and suddenly exclaimed she had lost her pin. When she said she would see the agent about another one, I knew that would not go over well. His strong reaction was "you had better find it"– and she did. Paul Crowley, our staff person cleaning restrooms, had found it, fortunately.

The security plan was to keep the president's destinations secret until the last minute to avoid crowds forming and increasing the security risk. In this case, we were instructed to block the entrance to Cadillac Summit ninety minutes before the family would arrive to prevent other visitors from going up. Then those visitors at the top would naturally leave after they saw the views without knowing the president was coming. This worked fine for about an hour, and then a few people noticed there were no more cars arriving and most of the parking lot was empty, an unusual occurrence for Acadia in June. On a hunch, some of these folks decided to stay. A few minutes before the motorcade arrived, the Secret Service used a wand to check each remaining person for a weapon and had them stand off to one side. Bomb-sniffing dogs went around each vehicle left in the lot. To the amazement of the small crowd, when the Obamas arrived, the president walked over to them and said hello, before returning to where Barb and I stood ready to welcome them to Acadia National Park.

There were agents with big binoculars and long guns stationed on each of the high points around the Cadillac summit. Obviously, they were there to defend against any threats from snipers or other shooters. The president also travels with a tactical team of specially trained agents, each equipped with sixty pounds of gear and ready to respond to any attack. Of course, the person carrying the "football," or the nuclear codes handcuffed to his wrist, was also near the president at all times.

Acadia's superintendent and wife greet the First Family on top of Cadillac Mountain.

Fortunately, the fog disappeared almost magically shortly before the family's arrival on top. After greeting them and posing for a quick photo, we walked around the summit path and the president remarked about the great beauty of Acadia and Maine. He said to me, "Wow, this would be a tough place to work."

The first family had flown into the small Bar Harbor airport in two smaller Air Force jets, not the usual 747. The plane carrying the president is always designated Air Force One no matter what size. Even the family dog, Bo, came along for the ride. The presidential limousine and other important support vehicles were flown into Bangor's larger airport inside big military transports. The official party, including numerous Secret Service agents and White House press corps, numbered more than 200 people. The presidential motorcade was made up of several security vehicles, the heavy armored limousine, the press vehicles, an ambulance, and various escort vehicles from the state and local police. Park rangers and local police formed the outer layer of security and usually were responsible for traffic control and manning road blocks.

Besides the hike at Ship Harbor, the views from Cadillac, and a bike ride and picnic on the Witch Hole loop of carriage road, the Obamas took a boat ride on the *Miss Ann*, the converted NPS lobster boat. The hour-long ride took the first family out into Frenchman Bay for a brief cruise among the islands. There were at least six U.S. Coast Guard gunboats surrounding us, and this security bubble moved as we moved. On board the park boat were President Obama, Michelle Obama, daughters Malia and Sasha, Valerie Jarrett, boat captain Tim Higgins, me, the White House advance person, a Secret Service agent, and a Coast Guard rescue swimmer. Ready for anything, the Coast Guard swimmer was in his wet suit and had already been in the water just to test the cold temperature and visibility. He was a highly trained individual who would dive into the worst possible conditions to save a life – certainly for the president and his family. Another diver had already checked the underside of our boat looking for any potential threats. Everyone enjoyed the boat ride, and the president was particularly interested in the lobster industry centered in this part of Maine. We also talked about the various islands that are part of Acadia and the economic impact of the national park. As we cruised back into Bar Harbor, the docks were lined with people yelling "We love you, Mr. President" and other nice things. I caught myself waving to the crowds like they were there for me, but quickly pulled my hand down realizing that was not the case. That rather awkward movement of mine was captured on the video I saw later that evening on CNN.

News photos showed me in uniform with a life jacket on so it wasn't long before the question was asked, "Why did the ranger (me) have a life jacket on, but not the first family?" Depending on who asked, I gave one of two possible answers for this question – one official and one unofficial. The official answer was that life jackets were readily available for each person on the boat (as required), and I was only wearing one as an example, hoping that everyone else might do the same. However, there was a rescue swimmer on board, an even better assurance that if the president or his family went overboard, the swimmer would instantly be there to save them. The unofficial answer was that had one of the Obamas gone overboard, the rescue swimmer would have immediately jumped in to save them and gotten them back on board; had I gone overboard, the swimmer would have said, "Oh, captain, you had better turn around. The superintendent just fell overboard."

Superintendent with Michelle and President Barack Obama on board the Miss Ann.

Sarah Vekasi, daughter of Acadia's chief of facilities management, called me prior to the Obamas' arrival to see if she might invite the president to her wedding, scheduled for the Saturday of the first family's visit. Her wedding was to take place at a private venue overlooking a small pond with the Seawall section of Acadia in the background. I explained that the family's schedule was already set, and I was sure he was not able to attend.

However, my wife and I did attend the wedding, and we sat looking at the bride standing with her back to the pond. On the other side of the pond was the road from Seawall Campground and the Ship Harbor Trail. Coincidentally, during the ceremony, the president's motorcade drove along that road on the other side of the pond. The wedding guests could clearly see the presidential party, and Sarah sensed from her guests' reaction to look toward the road, interrupting the ceremony to do so. The president saw a wedding in progress, and he waved as his car drove by. Sarah turned to the guests and exclaimed, "Yes! The president did come to my wedding after all!" Everyone clapped and waved to the Obamas enthusiastically.

— — — — — —

Acadia would not be a national park without the initial inspired work of George B. Dorr who spent his personal fortune buying land on Mount Desert Island for its permanent protection. Dorr and Charles Eliot established the Hancock County Trustees of Public Reservations in 1901 to preserve forest land and protect watersheds, and they began seeking land donations. In some other cases, Dorr used his own money to buy key parcels. Developers began to raise concerns about the amount of land being conserved, so they quietly went to the state legislature hoping to have the trustees abolished. Fortunately, Dorr learned of the effort and rushed to the state Capitol in time to defeat the measure. After averting this potential disaster, Dorr decided federal protection for the land would be more secure, so he traveled to Washington, D.C. in 1916. Having assembled more than 6,000 acres of protected land, Dorr appealed directly to President Woodrow Wilson. The president accepted the donation of 6,000 acres and established Sieur de Monts National Monument by presidential proclamation using the 1906 Antiquities Act. Dorr continued adding land, and in 1919 Congress enacted legislation changing the name to Layfette National Park.

George Dorr served as the first park superintendent for $1 per year until his death in 1944. He died almost penniless except for a little money his attorney had kept aside for his final arrangements. His body was to be cremated and his ashes spread over the national park. According to local legend, a group of women were having tea on their terrace when a small plane flew over, and something landed in a woman's cup of tea. The hostess reportedly said, "Oh, don't worry. Mr. Dorr was always dropping in unexpectedly."

Dorr's estate overlooked Compass Harbor where he built an ocean enclosure for swimming. Dorr frequently swam there no matter the temperature, which rarely gets above fifty-nine degrees even in the summer. The remains of his beautiful estate are still visible on his former property, which is now part of Acadia National Park. The only reminders of his once grand estate are stone stairways to the beach, part of the swim enclosure and remnants of his brick terrace. Someone on the park staff cleverly suggested that the loose bricks be stored for safekeeping to prevent people from taking them home to use as "Dorr stops."

One of George Dorr's greatest achievements was acquiring the only mainland part of Acadia – the Schoodic District. Nearly 2,200 acres on the end of Schoodic Peninsula were owned by John G. Moore and Dorr visited him about a possible donation of that land to become part of what was then Lafayette National Park. Moore seemed willing but passed away suddenly before any action was taken. Sometime later, Dorr visited Moore's two daughters who had inherited the land. Dorr told the daughters of his conversations with their father and asked if they might like to donate the land to the park in his memory. They said while they might consider that, they would never donate the land to a park "named after a Frenchman." Undeterred, this prompted Dorr to have the name changed to Acadia National Park in 1929. Subsequently, the daughters donated the extraordinary Schoodic land to Acadia. As a footnote, the new auditorium at Schoodic Institute was named the John G. Moore Auditorium in recognition of this tremendous gift.

While George Dorr was focused on land conservation, John D. Rockefeller Jr., also took a strong interest in Mount Desert Island. He was an experienced horseman who wanted to travel by horse and carriage on the Island roadways without encountering motor-driven vehicles. Between 1913 and 1940, Rockefeller not only began acquiring large blocks of land, but he decided to build a system of broken stone roads for use by horses and horse-drawn carriages. He hired the laborers and paid for the work, but more importantly, he spent many days overseeing the design and workmanship down to the smallest details. He wanted the roads to fit well with the natural surroundings, use local materials such as granite from the nearby Hall Quarry, and emphasize the natural beauty of Maine. The routes were chosen to include scenic vistas, rock outcroppings, stream crossings, and moderate grades along hillsides. Construction and landscaping were paid for and supervised by Rockefeller.

Probably the most interesting features of this system of scenic roads are the sixteen stone bridges. The first bridge was faced with cobblestones, and all the others are cut stone. Each bridge was designed by an architect to be unique. It took a stone mason crew a year or longer to build one bridge, and each one has the year of completion engraved into the stonework. Construction began with Cobblestone Bridge in 1917 and ended in 1933 with the Stanley Brook Bridge, my personal favorite with its gentle curves and three graceful arches.

Duck Brook Bridge, triple arch, cut stone completed in 1929.

The roads are lined with rectangular "coping stones," which add to the scenic quality of the roads. Today some locals refer to them as "Mr. Rockefeller's teeth." This seems like an appropriate term since the space between them must be periodically cleared to avoid small trees from growing into the macadam carriage roads. Hence, we have the term "flossing Mr. Rockefeller's teeth." John D. Rockefeller Jr. was also responsible for much of what we call the Park Loop

Road today. Both the fifty-seven miles of carriage roads and the Park Loop Road are listed on the National Register of Historic Places. As historic resources, park crews periodically thin trees and shrubs to preserve the important vistas along both the carriage roads and the Loop Road. Park management keeps a schedule for restoring or opening vistas as they tend to grow closed over time. It especially happens in Maine where there is significant rainfall each year, resulting in lush vegetation throughout the park.

Ultimately, John D. Rockefeller Jr. donated over 10,000 acres of land, including forty-five miles of carriage roads to become part of Acadia National Park. The Rockefeller family retained twelve miles of carriage roads and several thousand acres of land, but allowed public use to continue. Now forever preserved as historic structures, all the bridges are worthy of a bike ride or walk to see their unique character and design features.

Rockefeller also bought a sixty-room summer cottage with spectacular views of the Gulf of Maine and many nearby islands. He added another fifty rooms and magnificent gardens, calling his summer home the Eyrie, a fitting name given its perch high above the water. The Abby Aldrich Rockefeller gardens were named for his wife, and they continue to be a major attraction for tourists coming to Mount Desert Island. After Rockefeller died in 1960, the family decided not to continue to maintain the 110-room Eyrie and had it torn down in 1963. However, the terrace and gardens remain and are open to the public at certain times through the Mount Desert Land and Garden Preserve.

The Abby Aldrich Rockefeller gardens in Seal Harbor, Maine.

David Rockefeller Sr. maintained his summer home, Ringing Point, in Seal Harbor until his death in 2017 at age 101. He remained active up until the end, and I saw him driving his carriage on the family's beloved carriage roads regularly through the summer. One summer, I was invited to join him for lunch on *Sea Smoke*, his beautiful motor yacht, after which I gave him a tour of the recently renovated Schoodic Education and Research Center. It was a real treat to hear him talk about his father's work to develop the Loop Road and expand Acadia. David Rockefeller Jr. also has a summer home in Seal Harbor, and he is well known in the sailing community. The Rockefeller family continues to play a major role in land conservation and support for our national parks.

- - - - - -

I often use the term "checkerboard pattern" to describe Acadia's land ownership. While Acadia is made up of about 50 percent of the land on Mount Desert Island, the national park is a complicated jumble of public land and private properties. By contrast, Rocky Mountain National Park is a large rectangle with three entrances and exits, and almost all of the land inside is park protected. In addition to land from the four different towns on Mount Desert Island, Acadia includes pieces of about sixty islands and a large mainland piece on the Schoodic Peninsula. It is sometimes hard for visitors to know when they are in the park and when they are not.

The national park boundary is established by Congress through the legislative process. The official boundary map, which usually accompanies park specific legislation, defines what land is to be acquired by the National Park Service. Normally there is also legislative language that provides some specifics on any limitations or provisions for land acquisition in the park. Even older, longstanding national parks may still have private parcels within the boundary, called inholdings, that should be acquired through purchase or donation.

– – – – – –

Acadia is the only national park I know of that has two boundaries. There is the "fee acquisition" boundary where the National Park Service is mandated to acquire outright ownership of land. It totals about 37,000 acres. There is a much larger defined area where NPS can acquire conservation easements to protect scenic values of the park. Under a conservation easement, the landowner retains title to the property but agrees to certain use restrictions, which limit future development on the parcel. An easement can reduce the appraised value of the property and also lead to lower property taxes. The landowner either donates the easement, or in some rare cases the easement is purchased. Acadia has another 13,000 acres under conservation easement, and that number continues to slowly grow over time. The Acadia management staff includes a full-time land specialist who spends her time managing over 200 separate conservation easements and working on other potential donations. Clearly, Acadia's complex boundary and land management demands are greater than any other national park in this country.

Senator George Mitchell, former Senate majority leader, also has a summer home in Maine, and I would see him from time to time. He always told me the same thing: "Negotiating the park boundary for Acadia was more difficult than the Northern Ireland peace agreement." In addition to the Northern Ireland peace agreement, Senator Mitchell was the key person in writing and passing the legislation that established the Acadia National Park boundary in 1986. Prior to that, Acadia only had an unusual and loose "area of interest" for acquiring land to expand the park. Local officials, developers, and others wanted more certainty of where Acadia would acquire land and where it would not. Thus, they wanted to define and establish a permanent boundary. The many competing interests and the number of private landowners involved made it not only a complex issue but an emotional one for many people. Senator Mitchell called this one of the greatest challenges of his career. More details about land protection issues are in the following chapter.

- - - - - -

Democratic Senator Barbara Mikulski of Maryland came to Acadia for a few days one summer on an unofficial visit, but she did agree to speak at an annual meeting of the Schoodic Institute. Republican Senator Susan Collins of Maine was already set to be the keynote speaker, so Senator Mikulski spoke after her. Hearing the two senators speak and then answer questions from the audience was a treat. The two senators had great respect for each other even though they were from opposing parties.

Senator Mikulski is less than five feet tall, and her staff cautioned us to have step stools at the ready behind the podium and for any vehicles in which she might ride. Senator Mikulski was a senior member of the Senate Appropriations Committee. Therefore, it was a rare opportunity for me to give her a tour of Acadia and answer questions about federal funding and the growing challenges we faced as visitor numbers increased. I was particularly interested in obtaining for Acadia more money from the Land and Water Conservation Fund to buy critical parcels within the park boundary.

Since the Senator would be speaking at the Schoodic Education and Research Center, I thought it would be a good idea to show her land acquisition issues on the Schoodic Peninsula. The best viewpoint to understand the challenging ownership situation was the overlook on the backside of Schoodic

Head. The plan was to drive up to the parking lot near the top of Schoodic Head and walk from there, about one-third mile to the viewpoint. The most difficult part of that trail is the first one hundred yards, which climb up a broad granite slope with uneven surfaces. I offered Senator Mikulski my arm as we began slowly climbing the steep slope. We both realized that it was more difficult for her than I had hoped, and she turned to me and said, "Do you really think this is a good idea?" I immediately said, "No, I don't," and we turned around and headed back to the vehicle. Using a map and photos, I was able to explain how important it was to protect at least the southern half of the 3,200 acre Modena property. Senator Mikulski clearly supported our efforts to avoid severe degradation of the high-quality visitor experience in the Schoodic District of Acadia. I hoped the discussion might lead to some future funding.

— — — — — —

Secretary of the Interior, Dirk Kempthorne (appointed by President George W. Bush), came to Acadia as part of his effort to better understand Interior's field operations. We took the secretary on an auto tour of the park, and then he offered to meet with employees. We asked those employees who could break away from duty to come to our meeting room, called the "training trailer" since it was an old double-wide trailer placed on a foundation. Many rangers and maintenance workers remained on the job and missed this meeting, but about seventy-five staff and volunteers came to hear the relatively new secretary speak.

Prior to the meeting, I was chatting with Secretary Kempthorne in my office at park headquarters. On that day, it so happened we were going to honor our administrative officer, Mike Healy, for forty years of federal service. I asked Secretary Kempthorne if he would do the honors and present the length of service pin to Mike. Of course, he agreed but asked about Mike's history of service. I told him Mike had a great government career beginning in the CIA, followed by a decade with the Coast Guard. Mike then came into the National Park Service and joined the U.S. Park Police in Washington, D.C., as a motorcycle patrolman before coming to Acadia as the park's administrative officer.

As we were walking to the employee meeting, I saw Mike crossing the parking lot on his way to the training trailer, so I called Mike over to meet the secretary. After I introduced them, Secretary Kempthorne said to Mike, as if he knew a lot about him, "Mike Healy, Mike Healy, weren't you in the CIA?" Shocked and afraid his "secret" background was more common knowledge than it should have been, Mike said, "Hey, wait a minute. How do you know I was in the CIA?" We all laughed when I let Mike know I had just told the secretary about his interesting career history.

– – – – – –

We had another Interior secretary, Ken Salazar, visit us at Acadia. He was appointed under President Obama. We received a phone call from Washington telling us that Secretary Salazar wanted to come for a full day of touring and meeting employees at Acadia as part of an orientation visit to several Interior facilities in the East. For this trip, his new staff people wanted to make sure all details were in place for a good tour and meeting with park management. Several days ahead, they exchanged phone calls with Deputy Superintendent Len Bobinchock who planned and coordinated the itinerary for any visiting dignitary. Len and I often would spend the day with the visitor and introduce them to key staff during the tour to orient the person to the National Park Service's role in conservation and public service. These were great opportunities to discuss park needs and concerns, especially if the individual, such as a member of a congressional committee or high-level Department of the Interior official, was in a position to help address some of our challenges.

In this case, the new and likely inexperienced staffers wanted more detail. We started with an outline of stops during the tour, and they requested times be shown for each stop. They then asked us to assign specific times rather than blocks of time, so instead of Schoodic Education and Research Center - ninety minutes, they wanted SERC 9:20-10:45 and so forth. On the next more detailed itinerary, we showed sixty minutes for a boat ride from Schoodic to Bar Harbor so we could get across Frenchman Bay and show the secretary Acadia from the water, including various islands within the park boundary. It was also an excellent chance to discuss the need for more land acquisition money to buy properties that we were mandated to protect, such as Burnt Porcupine Island, one of the islands we would cruise by on the boat.

The secretary's staff in Washington called to say that sixty minutes for the boat trip was too long and we should cut the time by thirty minutes. We told them that the boat trip was from point A to point B on the water, and we couldn't reduce it, but they still insisted. So, the final itinerary showed thirty minutes less for the boat trip, which satisfied their demands. Of course, we knew that meant when we landed in Bar Harbor, we would be thirty minutes behind schedule. The final irony is that once we were all on the boat, which included the Washington staffers, the schedule no longer seemed to matter. It was a beautiful day on a lovely boat, and we were talking Interior business. This put everyone in a good mood. The lead scheduler said, "It's okay if we take more time cruising. This is great!"

Personally, I was frustrated because I had come down with laryngitis a few days before his visit. Even though I saved my voice for those days and did everything else the doctor recommended, I was still barely audible. However, I was able to make a few important points, and Len filled in the blanks, as always. We made a good team.

I was most impressed with Secretary Salazar, especially his interest and sincerity. At one point he asked what my top priorities were. That was an easy question to answer since I often recited my park goals to various audiences. I told him they were to protect the land within the park, improve service to visitors, make SERC a success, and engage youth. He asked for them in writing, so I wrote on a napkin, the only paper available at the time, and he put them in his pocket. Once in Bar Harbor, the secretary held a scheduled news conference, and at one point he pulled out the napkin and read my priorities. Then he said, "These are now Interior's priorities." Wow! Usually it takes months to get feedback from the secretary or director, and goals are more top down. As a footnote, I was amazed when a few months later I saw Secretary Salazar again in Washington, and he immediately recognized me and said, "Let me see if I can remember your goals for Acadia." He recalled three of the four without prompting. I believe Ken Salazar had great intentions for the Department of the Interior, but outside forces threw up roadblocks and, in the end, stymied his efforts and led to personal frustration. He retired back to Colorado after one term in the Obama administration. It was unfortunate for those of us interested in conservation results.

I will add however, that Sally Jewel followed Ken Salazar and she was also terrific! She too visited Acadia and met with employees. While a visit from the Secretary almost seems like a tradition, we often received visits from Washington officials because of Acadia's proximity to our nation's capital and it was a great place to visit.

Len and I would think about what we wanted to convey to dignitaries like the secretary, and this time we decided to focus on the increasing difficulty of hiring youth because of recent changes in government hiring policies. In the meeting we asked those in attendance under twenty-five to stand up, and then we asked those hired through the government process to remain standing. It left no one. All of the twenty or more youth who were employed were hired and paid for with private funding through Friends of Acadia.

Sally Jewell was an outstanding speaker, and we had arranged for her speech to a large audience of Acadia friends and supporters. Her remarks were well received, and the audience particularly enjoyed the opportunity to ask questions and hear in-depth answers. I think she returned to Washington favorably impressed with Acadia and our efforts to achieve the dual mission of the National Park Service: preservation while providing for visitor use and enjoyment.

– – – – – –

At the trail junction that leads to the Beehive, the sign reads "Caution: exposure and ladders ahead. If you have a fear of heights, this trail is not for you." One of the unique things about Acadia is its historic iron rung ladder trails. These trails were built by volunteer trail workers from the Village Improvement

Societies before 1916 when Acadia was first established as a national monument. Each of these ladder trails is unique, with names like Beehive, Jordan Cliffs, and the most challenging of all, the Precipice.

Barb thinks the Beehive is much easier than the other iron rung trails in Acadia. Sand Beach is far below.

I was sitting at the top of the Beehive one day watching as people finished the climb. Families, and particularly the kids, were excited to have completed this trail up the front of the dome-shaped mountain. Surprisingly, one college-aged woman completed the climb in a long dress and bare feet. Another young man was carrying his small dog in a front pack, although dogs are not permitted on the iron rung ladder trails. The dog probably didn't enjoy the experience as much as the people I saw that day.

A more explicit message near the beginning of the Precipice trail is on a yellow and black sign placed so that hikers cannot miss it. It reads: WARNING: *The Precipice is maintained as a non-technical climbing route, not a hiking trail. It follows a nearly vertical route with exposed cliffs that require climbing on iron rungs.*

Falls on this mountain have resulted in serious injury and death. Attempt this route only if you are physically fit, wearing proper footwear, and have experience in climbing near exposed cliffs, and heights.

Small children and people with fear of heights should not use this trail.

The warning is blunt but essential as the following story illustrates.

The much higher and longer Precipice route goes over and under rocks before scaling several ninety-degree cliff faces on iron rung ladders while gaining 1,100 feet of elevation on the east face of Champlain Mountain. Walking the narrow ledges with some significant exposure increases the scare factor, but at least there are iron railings to grasp for safety and assurance. Fortunately, people tend to be extra cautious because the dangers are obvious.

Not far from the parking lot that leads to the Precipice, hikers encounter their first obstacle: a large boulder with two iron rungs required to get up and over the rock. Those two rungs are uncomfortably spaced and too high for some people. Locally the rock is called "the eliminator" or the "intimidator," and it is hoped that people who struggle to get over it might think better about proceeding.

Some of the many iron rungs on the Precipice climbing route.

She said "It is only this wide up here!"

Ranger Richard Rechholtz tells the story of a man and wife who argued in the parking lot about going up the Precipice. She knew he was afraid of heights, and he indicated he really did not want to go. She badgered him until he reluctantly agreed, and finally off they went. About halfway to the top, where ladders and ledges seem to never end, he froze. He adamantly refused to go farther. Going down is not an option either; it is actually scarier looking down hundreds of feet, and hikers coming up find it hard to pass anyone going down. For these reasons, it is highly recommended people return from the top via a loop connector trail.

The wife left him there and went on to the top where she used her cellphone to call the rangers for help. Then she sat on top while her husband waited on a ledge below. Richard and another ranger took ropes and a harness up the trail until they reached the husband. The typical reaction when rangers arrive is: "We are so glad you are here" or "Thank goodness." In this case the man said, "Where the hell have you been?" The rangers ignored his ungrateful question, secured him in a harness, and helped him to the top where his wife was waiting impatiently. She immediately berated him. You can only imagine their exchange. As the party was heading down the connector trail, the wife tripped on her flip flops (never a good idea for hiking footwear) and broke her ankle. She then had to be carried out on a stretcher. Some on the park staff thought this evened the score between the two. Who knows if they are still married?

The Precipice is usually closed from March into August to protect nesting peregrine falcons. Even though this is a popular hike and climb, people support the need to protect the falcons and their young. If the nest fails to produce chicks, rangers open the trail sooner.

The spectacular view from the summit of Mount Champlain is reason enough to take one of several routes to the top, but I also liked to hang out up there and listen to the excitement and thrill of those completing the Precipice climb. Some people have climbed it multiple times. I have climbed the Precipice at least six to eight times with different friends, and it is always a great experience, unique in the national parks. My wife, on the other hand, has climbed it once — and that was enough. She said "Never again!"

Barb climbed the Precipice once and said "Never again!!"

We would never build such a trail today because environmentalists might say you should not put iron rungs on the cliff faces. People concerned with safety might express similar concerns. Since these trails predate the park, they are indeed historic, and therefore, we carefully maintain them as historic resources.

One time after a serious falling accident, I expected to get letters and calls to close the Precipice, but I was surprised to receive only letters and calls to keep it open. No one suggested closing it. However, in anticipation of receiving demands to close the Precipice, I analyzed the park's record of fatalities on various hiking trails to see if any one trail had significantly more than the others. Contrary to expectations, I learned that serious accidents were widely distributed over the park's many trails, including those without ladders. Outdoor enthusiasts accept some level of risk as we all do going about our daily lives (driving, flying, biking, or just sitting at home), and visiting national parks is no exception. We probably could eliminate almost all risk to park users, but many would not enjoy the bland and tightly controlled experience.

— — — — — —

In addition to the iron rung ladders, Acadia is known for the beautiful stonework on many of the hiking trails. Our trail crews are skilled at building intricate and practical stone bridges, steps, and drains made from local granite. The crews do almost all hand work, and they use cables and pulleys to move granite, which weighs 168 pounds per cubic foot, around the work site. They often have used stones that are several cubic feet in volume, which means it takes both strength and engineering to get them into place. With work sites often miles from the nearest trailhead, granite is usually taken from a nearby remote spot out of sight of trail users. Crews also drill and break the stone into the desired size and shape right at the site, using the same techniques developed a hundred years ago. Granite fractures in near rectangular shapes resulting in attractive steps and coping stones used along trails and carriage roads.

Many trails, such as Perpendicular and Homan's Path, have beautiful stone steps and retaining walls. Perpendicular, as the name implies, goes pretty much straight up in places and has more than 500 cut stone steps. The stonework on the Perpendicular is indeed of the highest quality and one of my favorite examples of Civilian Conservation Corps work at Acadia. One young boy asked trail workers if the glaciers left the stone in those patterns. I think he was kidding, but we do get some unusual questions.

Acadia's 130 miles of trails are maintained mostly with private funding that comes from a Friends of Acadia endowment. With severely constrained budgets, we likely would not be maintaining the trails to a high standard without this significant help. In addition, Acadia Youth Conservation Corp, Student Conservation Association, and other volunteers work alongside our crews or do other, perhaps less intricate, trail work. Fortunately, using all of these sources of labor, we are able to get much more work done with less impact to the park's limited budget.

— — — — — —

Reconstruction of some trail segments happens each year with projects programmed several years in advance. Most people do not realize the pre-work involved, including collecting and saving native plant material near the project site, and collecting the leaf litter and pine needle duff so it can be put back after the project is completed. This way the scars from construction disappear almost immediately. Finally, all trails must be surveyed early each season to find downed trees to remove, broken or missing bridge planks to replace, or loose iron rungs and railings that might present safety concerns. Dealing with safety issues becomes the highest priority in the early season workload.

— — — — — —

The history of Acadia's extensive system of trails dates back to 1891 when the first trail plans were drafted. Most of the trail construction was coordinated by Village Improvement Societies made up of local volunteers. One fresh approach to trail funding at the time was to allow donors who financed a particular trail to name it after a person of their choice. One example was Kurt Diederich's Climb on Dorr Mountain. Plaques were often erected along these trails with the name of the person so honored, and these plaques remain today.

According to The History of Acadia's Trails: "Waldron Bates, chair of the Roads and Paths Committee of the Bar Harbor Village Improvement Association from 1900 to 1909, was the first to incorporate stone stairways and iron rung ladders into trails to traverse cliffs, talus slopes, and other steep areas." An example of his work is Gorham Mountain's Cadillac Cliffs Trail. A plaque at the head of the trail memorializes Bates as "Pathmaker."

The History of Acadia's Trails continues: "Others who followed Waldron Bates carried on his legacy of innovation and craftsmanship. Rudolph Brunnow built the Precipice Trail over the formerly impassable cliffs of Champlain Mountain, and George Dorr, one of Acadia's founders and the park's first superintendent, promoted memorial paths. He oversaw the construction of several stairway trails leading from Sieur de Monts Spring to the summit of the mountain that now bears his name."

Homan's Path, the Emery Path, and the Schiff Path are wonderful short trails on Dorr Mountain that convey a real beauty of design and construction. In addition, from late July through August hikers can find an abundance of wild blueberries along these trails, which certainly sweeten the experience.

Another passage from the book says "The Great Depression brought the New Deal and the Civilian Conservation Corps (CCC) to Acadia National Park. Two camps were established on the island in 1933, one on McFarland Hill (now park headquarters), and the other just south of Long Pond on the west side of the island. A good deal of CCC work involved trails. East-side crews primarily rehabilitated existing trails constructed by village improvement societies. West-side crews expanded the trail system on newly acquired tracts along Western Mountain. The Perpendicular and Great Pond Trails are examples of work completed by the CCC." Most recently, the top part of the Perpendicular was re-done by Acadia's trail crew.

Acadia's historic trails are still as challenging to present-day hikers as to those of generations past, and their scenic values and ties to the landscape evoke the same sense of awe and inspiration experienced long ago.

- - - - - -

This boy on a nature cruise never looked up.

The boy never looked up. We were on a nature cruise out of Northeast Harbor. Harbor porpoise were jumping out of the water, bald eagles flying by, and an osprey sat in its nest with chicks. Visitors were hoping to see whales and other exciting marine life and seabirds. The ranger was telling us interesting information about marine mammals. He also discussed significant ocean trends that have major consequences for those mammals, and for the regional economies, tourism, area communities, and our marine environment. The boy, about eight, with his hoodie pulled up, was sitting between his parents and playing on his hand-held device. I don't think he saw or heard a thing other than what was on his screen. Had I been his parent, I would have been tempted to confiscate the Game Boy or even throw it overboard.

Getting youth outdoors and engaged with nature has long been a personal goal of mine. As mobile phones and the internet consume more time in the life of today's young people, I have grown increasingly concerned about the future of conservation, the environment, and national parks. When children are focused on a hand-held device, everything around them seems to become irrelevant.

A growing body of research indicates that kids who regularly spend time outdoors gain substantial benefits. They do better in science and math, they are more creative thinkers, they are less stressed and less obese, and they are generally heathier both physically and emotionally. I also think people who regularly spend time outdoors are more engaged in the world around them, the real world. Nature appeals to all your senses, not just one. If people grow up consumed by their mobile phone world, who will care about the neighborhood or the quality of the air and water, or society's needs and challenges?

Working with the Friends of Acadia, we developed several youth programs that get kids into the park and fully engaged in the natural environment. The Acadia Youth Conservation Corps, Ridge Runners, Cadillac Summit Stewards, and High School Tech Team all present great opportunities for youth to spend up to eight weeks working alongside Acadia staff. Friends of Acadia paid them with donated funds.

The Youth Tech Team is made up of four to six high school students and a young adult leader. They are hired by Friends of Acadia, but they work closely with the park's professional staff. Their focus is on two things. For the first few weeks, they get to know the national park through observation and participation in ranger-led programs, tours, and working with the trail crew and rangers for short assignments. For the second half of the summer, they are then asked to help us develop new ways of reaching their peers through technology or other approaches. At the conclusion of their summer's work, they present their recommendations to the park staff. An example of their ideas that Acadia implemented was a "falcon cam" video camera focused on a clifftop peregrine falcon nest. Visitors can view recorded segments on a monitor set up at the parking lot below. Education rangers can replay the most interesting or exciting scenes, such as hatching or feeding, for visitors who otherwise might not see much bird activity when they stop at the roadside peregrine viewing site. These observers can also get the big picture of where the nest is, when a parent flies in or out, and when a parent returns with food. The close-up videos are more interesting and meaningful since the nest is just above.

We heard from the participants that these multi-week youth programs have a significant impact on their young lives. We hear statements like this: "This summer has changed my life," or "I hope to be a park ranger now," or "Acadia has always been nearby but it never meant much to me personally until now." It is great to hear these and other similar comments about their positive experiences in Acadia National Park. We are fortunate to have donated funds available to develop excellent youth programs like these that benefit both the youth and the National Park Service.

— — — — — —

After a meeting in downtown Bar Harbor, I was walking up the street to my car. Easily recognizable in uniform, people often stop me to ask a question or offer a comment about Acadia or other national parks. On this particular day, two young boys across the street were getting into a car with their family, and they yelled over to me in unison, "Hey, ranger." I looked over, and they together yelled again proudly, "We are junior rangers," and showed me their junior ranger hats. I loved their enthusiasm and pride.

The Junior Ranger Program is another great way to engage even younger kids. They get a free booklet at any national park office or visitor center, and then they complete the booklet during their visit. They answer a few questions, attend one ranger program, and when their workbook is completed, they turn it in at the national park visitor center. A park ranger enthusiastically announces to those visitors in the center that Acadia has a new junior ranger, and everyone applauds. Our rangers publicly recognize over 1,000 new junior rangers each summer in Acadia, with many of them proudly wearing their junior ranger badges home. The program stimulates young interest in national parks and the environment, and it results in lasting memories of worthwhile summer experiences.

About to complete his junior ranger workbook.

- - - - - -

Even when I was not in uniform, I was often recognized in small town Bar Harbor. People would sometimes ask me a park question or make a comment about Acadia or national parks when I was at the grocery store or pharmacy. One evening my wife and I were out to dinner with friends at Fiddlers Green in Southwest Harbor. Our server, a young man named Darren, asked me if I was the superintendent of Acadia, and I said yes. He proudly said his father was the trails foremen, and I said of course I knew him, and his father was a terrific leader for Acadia's trails program. While we waited for our dinners, actress Susan Sarandon walked in and was seated nearby. We occasionally saw celebrities around Bar Harbor, and Susan had visited Maine during other summers too. As we were leaving, the owner of the restaurant said to me, "Hey, I have to tell you something." She said our server had come up to her all excited and said, "Do you know who is in the restaurant tonight?" and she replied "Yes, Susan Sarandon," but the server responded "No, the superintendent of Acadia!" I got a hearty laugh from that, and it was good for the ego too.

At another time in the Bangor airport while waiting for a flight, a woman was a few seats away reading the Friends of Acadia Journal. She was on the page where my regular column appears along with my photo. She looked at me and then pointed to the photo and then me and said, "Is that you?" I said yes, and she went on to tell me about how much she loved Acadia. It reminded me that I should always be on my best behavior because I couldn't assume I was anonymous anywhere in Maine.

– – – – – –

One summer Acadia had a visit from a group of protected area managers from Italy. We gave them a tour of the park and talked at length about park operations, our major challenges, and how we deal with them. Maurilio Cipriano, an environmental activist, and Dino Martino, the director of Dolomiti National Park in Italy, led the group. By the end of the visit, we had agreed that Acadia would be a sister national park to Dolomiti. While our natural resources were different, ocean coastline versus dramatic mountains, many of our challenges and issues were similar, and we could learn from each other. The delegation from Italy was particularly impressed with our park budget, our Friends of Acadia group and the private money it raises, and our volunteer program. They said developing community support groups and volunteerism are things that are not even possible in Italy today.

Acadia's planner points out the 3200 acres threatened
by development on the Schoodic Peninsula.

As part of our tour for the delegation, I took them to Schoodic Head overlook to show them a large piece of land owned by a family from Italy. Standing
on that high point with the great view, I emphasized the potential for significant
negative impacts to Acadia if that private land was developed. I told them I was
having a difficult time learning more about the owners, and Maurilio offered
to try to find out more about them when he returned home.

Soon after that visit led by Maurilio Cipriano, I was invited to come to
Visso, Italy, just outside of Sibillini National Park, to speak to a group of about
sixty protected area managers from throughout Italy. I was honored to make
that presentation, which highlighted how we manage national parks in the
United States and how much we depend on private philanthropy and volunteers.
Overall, these managers were amazed by Acadia's operating budget and staff size.
They were also impressed by how much freedom local managers have, and the
availability of volunteers and private funding. I remarked at how many retirees
in the U.S. are eager to continue active lifestyles, including volunteering in the
parks. One person responded that in Italy, when one retires, they typically go
home and spend the rest of their days in a rocking chair. Volunteering is not

219

popular in Italy. National parks in Italy are fairly autonomous, with no central government office, but they are subjected to local politics to a much greater degree. As part of this official trip to Italy, I was welcomed by the U.S. Embassy in Rome and given a short briefing on things to know about the country. One particularly important piece of advice was in Italy, "drivers take speed limits and other official road signs as suggestions", and to be extra careful on curvy roads because motorcyclists are often passing in the middle. This advice proved to be important, and driving a rental car in Italy became an unforgettable experience.

About a year after the Italian delegation visited Acadia, my wife and I and another couple traveled to Italy to visit Dolomiti National Park, our new sister park. Unfortunately, Dino Martino had been forced from his director's position for political reasons, and we ended up meeting with the board president for Dolomiti, a person who seemed to have little interest in the sister park concept. However, we did have a good tour of their park and facilities over three days. As we concluded our second day of touring their park, we were told that the rangers wanted to take us up into the mountains and show us a new ranger station. They would pick us up at our hotel early the next morning.

Three rangers came to our hotel in their handsome uniforms and three small cars (Suzukis). I was escorted to the first vehicle and introduced to the chief ranger by our Italian guide. My wife got in the second car, and the other couple got in the third car. We started off through a nearby small town and then approached a locked gate across what looked like a two-track dirt road. The chief ranger got out and unlocked the gate, got back in and started driving but without putting his seat belt on again. Soon he said, "I see you have your seat belt on. You should take it off." I soon found out why as we climbed steeply on a two-track road that became a one-track, narrow mountain trail. It took us three hours to go less than five miles, all uphill and carefully. We probably could have walked up in the same amount of time. Actually, my wife would have preferred hiking to riding in a small car with a driver who did not speak English.

The chief ranger explained that only three entities could use this trail and only one at a time. There was no possibility for passing or getting off the road, out of the way of another vehicle. There were no turnouts or turnarounds and having one vehicle back up was also out of the question. The road had a thin "fence" consisting of one strand of wire on one-inch diameter poles along parts of the road with the most exposure. This flimsy fence could never stop a vehicle from going off a cliff, but rather it would serve as a vital warning if the car scraped it.

The road had many tight switchbacks that required even these small vehicles to back up several times to get around the corner. Backing up had to be done carefully or the car could back off the edge; hence the reason for not wearing seat belts – in case we had to jump out quickly. We did stop occasionally to talk and to take photos. The route was so nerve-wracking that as we neared the top, Barb asked one of the English-speaking rangers if she could walk the rest of the way -- and she did.

Above the clouds, returning from our visit to an
Italian ranger station in the Dolomites.

Finally, we arrived at a refugio, a place where hikers could spend the night or get a meal. We left our cars there and walked the last mile to the ranger station. Once there, the rangers asked us to wait outside the new, but shuttered, building while they opened it to let light in. We then were invited in and given a quick tour of the bunk room, kitchen area, and the common room. The chief ranger pointed to a large oak dining table in the main room and invited us to sit down. The rangers brought out several bottles of wine and enough glasses for everyone. It was still not 11 a.m., but a glass or two of wine seemed both customary and a nice way to calm our nerves. As we sat, talked, and drank wine, I could only think of driving back down that road, or should I say trail? About an hour later we went back to the refugio for lunch and more wine. I put my faith in the fact that these guys drink lots of wine, and they certainly knew the dangers of the route up and down the mountain. It was quite the adventure and an experience we will never forget.

— — — — — —

The superintendent of Acadia National Park is also superintendent of Saint Croix Island International Historic Site, about a two-hour drive north of Acadia. Saint Croix Island is in the middle of the Saint Croix River, which forms the border between Canada and the United States. The historic site is the island that Samuel Champlain first landed on in 1604, and some of his party remained on that island through one winter. Many of those men died that winter and are buried there. Champlain moved the remaining men north into what is today Canada. Had the island become the first permanent settlement in America, it would have held that distinction instead of Jamestown, Virginia.

As a speaker to a large organization in southern Maine, I was introduced with the title of superintendent of both Acadia National Park and Saint Croix International Historic Site. After the program one person remarked that I had the best job they ever heard of, thinking I spent half a year in Maine at Acadia and half a year in the Virgin Islands. He had confused the role with Saint Croix Historic Site in the Caribbean. I told him with the winters in Maine, I could only wish for such a combination, but Saint Croix International Historic Site is two hours north of Acadia near the Canadian border.

— — — — — —

One final personal note: I am often asked which park assignments was my favorite. My response is always that I loved each one but for different reasons. I was truly fortunate to be able to work at something I had great passion for

– national parks, conservation, and serving the American public. I stayed at Acadia for over 12 years because I loved the combination of natural beauty, historical interests, public support, and the many partners, donors, and volunteers who worked to make Acadia such a magnificent experience for both visitors and park staff. During my years at Acadia, I could have taken other assignments, but I wondered why would I want to start over again in another park when Acadia had all of the ingredients for challenging and rewarding work. A perfect job was made even better by working with the many dedicated and hardworking park employees, volunteers, and partners that keep Acadia such a special place.

CHAPTER EIGHT

"BUY LAND, THEY AIN'T MAKING ANY MORE OF IT." -- WILL ROGERS

Except for real estate agents and land conservation enthusiasts, most people probably think the topic of land acquisition seems boring. However, when you are preserving land that contains significant natural or historical resources, or tracts of land that are important missing pieces of national parks, the topic can be exciting. I call the need to preserve those missing pieces "filling in the holes," which is a simple concept that people understand. These are parcels inside authorized park boundaries that the National Park Service has been directed to acquire, but for one reason or another, they still remain in private ownership. Even parks that are over 100 years old, like Rocky Mountain and Acadia, have inholdings that need to be acquired as opportunities arise. In cases where private properties inside park boundaries become threatened with an incompatible use, the need to acquire is much more urgent.

Land is the essence of any national park because it is the land that contains the natural and cultural features that people come to enjoy. Owning the land is the best way to permanently protect park values for present and future generations. My passion has always been for national parks and the National Park Service mission: preserving essential park resources and encouraging people to enjoy their national parks.

When you think about the bad things that can happen to these nationally significant resources if they are not protected, such as subdividing the land and building houses and roads, tearing down historic structures, destroying wildlife habitat, clearing trees, developing mining operations, or filling in wetlands, you get the idea. These are examples of land uses that are clearly incompatible with protected areas such as national parks. It is vital to protect the land and resources inside and adjacent to national parks before the resources are damaged or destroyed. Equally important are what I call the "spillover effects" when use of a private parcel negatively impacts the surrounding public land. Examples would be air, water, noise or light pollution coming from the private properties that then spill on to the parkland, which degrades the natural values or the visitor experience in the immediate area. For all of these reasons, land protection was my highest priority throughout my career.

Bass Harbor Marsh where a donor purchased two
threatened parcels and gave them to the park.

– – – – – –

When I first arrived at Acadia, I spent a few days riding around with Mike Blaney, the park's land specialist. I soon learned that there were more than twenty parcels within the park boundary that were for sale by willing sellers, but we could not buy them due to a lack of funding. A few of the parcels were developed with cabins or other structures, but most were undeveloped and generally in a natural condition. A timely purchase would assure that the undeveloped tracts would remain that way and not present private use conflicts within the park. Buying these available properties was particularly important, both to preserve the natural character of Acadia and to prevent possible greater impacts in the future.

In 1964, the Land and Water Conservation Fund (LWCF) was established by law to purchase land for both federal agencies and state parks. Each year, Congress appropriates money from that fund with a portion of it allocated to national parks for land purchase. Every year there is much more land to buy than money allocated. The demand clearly outstrips the available land purchase money appropriated through the normal process. Therefore, I began to look for other sources of money for land acquisition that could supplement any LWCF funds we might get from Congress.

The national park, Friends of Acadia, and Maine Coast Heritage Trust entered a three-way partnership to raise private money and negotiate purchases for some of the twenty-plus parcels of private land that were for sale. I was especially concerned about the undeveloped land that could be built upon in ways that would be incompatible with park protection and enjoyment. Preserving open space and natural habitat were obvious objectives when Congress established Lafayette National Park in 1919 and in the Acadia legislation of 1929 and 1986.

One of the state's well-known conservationists was Roxanne Quimby (the founder of Burt's Bees) who had a house in Winter Harbor just across the bay from Bar Harbor. Roxanne was quietly buying large pieces of forest land in northern Maine, near Mount Katahdin and Baxter State Park, with the objec-

227

tive of creating another national park in Maine. Early on, I met Roxanne and we would often spend time talking about land conservation and what was going on in Maine and especially Acadia. During one conversation, we had stopped in the park at a pull off overlooking Otter Cove, a particularly scenic spot. The natural scene of the water surrounded by trees with a mountain backdrop was interrupted by only one man-made structure with its roof above the trees. I explained to her that the one house was on a parcel that the park hoped to acquire someday. When the opportunity arose, Roxanne bought that property and had the house removed before giving the land to Acadia. She became the fourth partner in our land protection team. She ultimately purchased 10 parcels totaling about 500 acres making it look "easy" compared to how slow it was for the National Park Service to get funding and arrange purchases. Maine Coast Heritage Trust bought a few key parcels and NPS received some LWCF funding to buy others. Using this four-way partnership, we acquired 31 parcels inside the park boundary that could have been developed in ways contrary to the park's purpose. They were potential threats that have been taken off the park's priority "to do" list and those parcels now belong to all Americans.

Personally, an equally important focus was on reducing the threat of incompatible land use along the park boundary where development of private property immediately adjacent to parkland could also negatively impact park values. Because Acadia had the secondary authority to obtain conservation easements outside of the park's purchase area, we could enlist the assistance of either Friends of Acadia or Maine Coast Heritage Trust to protect important properties outside the primary boundary. In fact, Acadia's conservation easement program covered more than 200 properties and some 13,000 acres. The easement program was an important component of our land protection success.

At every opportunity, I would tell people the "single most serious threat to Acadia is the 3,200-acre tract of undeveloped private land that jutted into the Schoodic District" of the park. This important private parcel was outside the park boundary on the Schoodic Peninsula, and therefore, the NPS had no authority to buy this tract. While we did have authority to obtain a conservation easement, most developers had no interest in placing restrictions on their property which would limit its future use potential. This property was in the name of Winter Harbor Holding Company LLC, and contact information was not readily available. If this large property were developed, it would have resulted in tremendous damage to that beautiful part of Acadia.

The Schoodic District, the only part of Acadia on the mainland, is extraordinarily scenic with spectacular coastline, several beautiful islands just offshore, and rugged terrain of granite outcrops. High points and open areas provide great vistas of Frenchman Bay, Cadillac Mountain, and the ever-changing Gulf of Maine.

Looking at Little Moose Island from the Schoodic
Peninsula coastline. Rugosa Rose in bloom.

– – – – – –

As agreed, I stood under the Legal Sea Foods restaurant sign in Boston's Logan Airport, waiting for the right stranger to approach me to begin our long-anticipated meeting. I wondered what he would look like. How good was his English? And how would we identify each other and begin a conversation that I long thought would never happen? Let me start at the beginning of this amazing story.

Soon after transferring to Acadia National Park from Black Canyon in Colorado, I spent time reviewing land ownerships in and around the park boundary to better understand challenges or threats in accomplishing our mission. That mission, established in law, clearly states that park managers must work to preserve the natural and cultural values of national parks for present and future generations – a tall order.

I had become particularly concerned about the 3200 acres of developable land that had national park land on three sides of it in some places. The natural beauty, unique character, and special experiences on the Schoodic Peninsula would be forever diminished if this property were developed with incompatible land uses. I could imagine how hundreds of houses, suburban streets, street-lights, and traffic would degrade the natural environment in and around the park and completely change the charm and character of sleepy Winter Harbor.

When faced with a major threat to a national park such as Acadia, my first instinct was to learn more about the land involved and particularly the owner(s). Especially in this case, with the property's sheer size, proximity to the existing parkland, and potential for large-scale development, the importance of taking action was apparent. Contacting and meeting the owner became a major part of the challenge. There was some indication that the name Bruno Modena of somewhere in Italy was tied to the property. The true owners and their contact information seemed to be purposely obscured. An internet search turned up nothing of value. I even asked the U.S. Embassy in Rome to see if they could learn more about Bruno Modena. But I had little success and obtained no new information.

The Winter Harbor Holding Company land included more than a mile of beautiful granite shoreline, two pristine islands, an important wildlife corridor, and high vantage points with sweeping views of picturesque islands and the mountains beyond. The owners seemed to be hiding under layers of protection, resisting all attempts to talk to people who might oppose plans to develop the property without considering the potential negative impacts to one of America's most popular national parks.

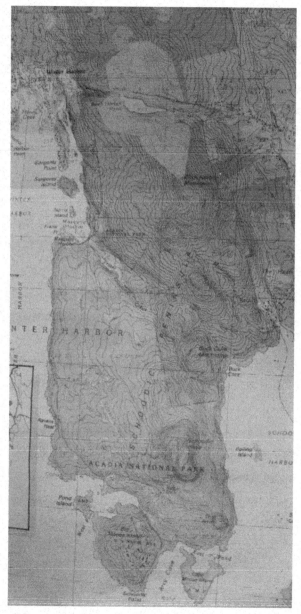

The darker shaded area adjacent to Acadia is part of 3,200 acres threatened by massive development.

Often local planning officials become aware of discussions by the owners or their representatives, and rumors begin to spread. Sometimes the owners are interested in selling, which seems like the best solution for all parties unless the asking price is beyond reasonable. In this case, it was apparent that the owners were not interested in conservation, but intent on large-scale development to produce the most return on their investment.

We heard from a contact in the governor's office that Bruno Modena and his son, Vittorio, had called and talked to the governor about this land. This outreach at least confirmed who we were dealing with. Soon after, and despite the worldwide economic downturn, the Modenas hired a group of land planning consultants from New York. The planners initially met with my staff and me at the park as an early gesture of cooperation, but they couldn't tell us much about owner intentions. Not long after that, we began to hear rumors of a massive real estate development, including hundreds of villas, three resorts, a golf course, and even an airstrip.

I initiated a number of steps to oppose this development, including having our crew build a short trail to an overlook above the Modena property. We erected a sign to guide people to the overlook, and soon Friends of Acadia began taking people to that viewpoint to build public understanding of the threat and its potential negative impacts to Acadia. We encouraged stories and editorials by the news media that would let the owners know of the widely supported efforts to protect Acadia. Quarterly meetings were held at park headquarters to bring together area conservation leaders and others who would work in collaboration to aggressively defend Acadia. At one time, Maine Coast Heritage Trust bought a conservation easement on a key parcel preventing the Modenas from adding that property to their development. All of this demonstrated our resolve in preventing the massive development that the owners intended. We also continued attempting to make contact with the Modenas and to arrange a meeting, even if a delegation would need to travel to Italy. No luck.

After a year or more of secretive activity, the planning team announced a public meeting in Winter Harbor, population about 250 in the winter. Given the tract's size and its prominence on the peninsula, many locals shared the park's concern about future development plans. Rumors about a large development of villas and resorts resulted in a huge turnout. It seemed that most of the town residents showed up at the school for the largest public meeting audience anyone could recall. The plans received a cool reception, and many questions went unanswered that night. However, a few vocal attendees wanted to see the development go forward, saying it would help improve the local economy and produce much-needed jobs. On the other hand, many others opposed the development and wanted the community to remain as it was, a quiet fishing village. Others thought there could be some middle ground that would help the economy without destroying the unique beauty and character of the area.

This public meeting gave me a chance to meet the new project manager, Cecilia Ward from Florida. I told her I would like to meet the owners when possible. She was vague about such an opportunity. After all, her paycheck would stop if the land was purchased or preserved.

Soon after, I was showing a delegation of land managers from Italy around the park and took them to the overlook that demonstrated how important the Italian-owned land was to the national park. The group leader, Maurilio Cipriano, later discovered that a friend at Haifa University knew Vittorio Modena who taught at Haifa for a few years. Some weeks later, I was surprised when the project manager from Florida called me and said, "I understand you wish to meet with Mr. Modena." She said that could be arranged if I were willing to travel to Boston the following week. I was scheduled to be in Washington, D.C. then but immediately changed plans to get to Boston's Logan Airport under that sign. I chose that spot because it would be hard to confuse its location given there was only one such place in the sprawling airport. Since we had never met, it was going to be an interesting meeting full of uncertainties, but I hoped it might lead to some new possibilities. We sat in the food court and talked for an hour and a half. Fortunately, Mr. Modena spoke fluent English.

I began by telling him of my three goals for our meeting: One, to establish and maintain contact with him as the landowner of a property that could significantly alter the future of Acadia National Park; two, to inform him that if the family wanted to sell the property, I was confident conservation interests in Maine would raise the money to purchase it; and three, to encourage him to meet with a conservation-minded developer, the Lyme Timber Company. This company had a solid record of developing sensitive properties near conserved lands in ways that were compatible with the values of those protected areas. I gave him the name of Peter Stein, one of the principals of Lyme Timber.

Vittorio replied that they were not interested in selling the land, but if they were, it was "probably worth $200 million dollars." After the initial shock, I said if that were the price, we could never raise that amount. He then qualified his estimate: "It would be worth that amount if all of our plans were approved and ready to go." He went on to say that "In its present, undeveloped state, it was probably worth $50 million." I thought to myself that this number was still unrealistic, but at least the numbers were going the right way – down.

I asked him if they would split the land into two parcels, thinking that the south half (as divided by State Route 86) was the most ecologically and visually important, containing the key coastal land and islands. He said he would think about that and get back to me, but he really didn't think the family had any interest in selling. We departed with each other's email addresses and phone numbers, and new hope that ultimately, we might be able to either influence the development plans to reduce negative impacts or better yet, conserve major portions of it.

About the same time, the world economy was in serious trouble. Many building projects in the United States had stopped or slowed. Banks were not lending money as before, and as the financial gains from developing properties declined, the prospects for purchasing lands for conservation seemed to be improving in general. I could only hope that these trends might help us in our fight to save the special character of the Schoodic Peninsula.

Meanwhile, with our conservation partners, we continued the campaign to raise public awareness of this major threat to Acadia, building support for preserving at least the southern half of the property. The next time I heard from

Vittorio Modena, he had evidently consulted with the family and said, "To my surprise, the family might be interested in selling ... for the right price." Of course, the price was always the big hurdle when developers are involved. I was also pleased to hear him put separate prices on various pieces of the land, all of which added up to $29 million. The south half alone was priced at $19 million because of the ocean frontage, the islands, good road access, and the fact that adjacent national park land was forever protected. The park provided spectacular scenic views and recreational opportunities for prospective private homeowners.

The Modenas also contacted Peter Stein of Lyme Timber Company as I had suggested. It appeared that the Modenas were hoping that Lyme Timber might become a major investor and provide the money needed to develop the project. It seemed that the Modena family hoped that their investment would be limited to the value of the land.

Lyme Timber representatives knew of the national park interest in preserving the land, and they hoped to work toward a negotiated purchase of some or all of the Modena property. Lyme Timber often played the role of interim buyer for conservation groups by purchasing and holding important parcels while private funding was raised to permanently secure the property. The only disadvantage of this approach was the additional holding costs that increased the amount needed to be raised.

Peter Stein of Lyme called me one day to say they were working hard on the Modenas, and they thought they might be able to buy the whole property and hold it until conservation interests could raise the money to buy it from them. With holding costs, legal fees, and a return on their investment, he thought it could be purchased and held for several years for around $17 million. While the price continued to go in the right direction, I knew it would be difficult to raise that much money, particularly with the added holding costs and return on investment or profit.

Not long after that, in August, I was at a cocktail party when someone asked me about bicycling in Acadia. The individual wanted to know where people could ride bikes and which route was my personal favorite. I replied that while all forty-five miles of carriage roads inside the national park were enjoyable for bike riding, I preferred to ride the park road over on the Schoodic Peninsula. I said "It is one of the most scenic roads in the country. The paved road is two lanes, one way and lightly traveled, unlike the roads in the main part of Acadia on Mount Desert Island. The only negative is the fact that once you leave the park road on the opposite side of the peninsula, you have to ride on busy State Highway 186 to get back to your starting place." I told him that someday I would like to close the loop inside the park to make the whole bike riding experience safer and more enjoyable. He asked me what it would take to complete that loop, and I said the big obstacle preventing a connecting bike path was that a family in Italy owned the land where the best connection would go.

He asked if the land could be purchased and what it was worth. I said that it was part of 3,200 acres of land owned by the Modena family of Milan, Italy, and that I didn't know the appraised value. I also told him that the land was extremely important to the park and it was currently threatened with development. I added that the land was probably worth at least $10 million. The man immediately replied, "I could do that."

More than a little surprised, I was not sure if he was just making conversation, or if he actually might be willing to buy it for that amount. I continued talking up the importance of the property. Finally, he said he had a family foundation, and he could buy the property if it were for sale.

Excitedly, I went home and put together a package of maps and other information on the 3,200 acres and took them to his house the next day. The following Monday, I called Peter Stein at Lyme Timber and asked him what the land might cost if I could find the money "up front." Stein said such an approach would eliminate holding costs and return on investment, and they would do the transaction for their costs plus the purchase price, maybe $15 million or less.

The friend with the foundation made it clear from the start that the family was to remain strictly anonymous if they got involved. I put the potential donor in touch with Peter Stein at Lyme Timber, and a few months later I received a call saying that they had purchased the property for less than $15 million --

and it would close in December. I was amazed and thrilled that this key property would now be protected forever. It was a great illustration of how private individuals could act much faster and be nimbler compared to the slower governmental process. Normally, an NPS purchase would require an appraisal, a National Environmental Policy Act analysis, and NPS approval from above. In addition, every NPS project would have to compete for funding with the land acquisition needs for all national parks around the country. Funding would have to come from a congressional appropriation or from a conservation organization after a private fundraising campaign. All these steps could take years, and in the meantime, the opportunity could be lost. In this situation, NPS or a conservation group would normally try to secure an option on the property for up to three years, allowing enough time to line up funding and finalize the purchase without damage to the land.

This inability to act quickly to take advantage of important opportunities is the primary reason we seek to build partnerships with private nonprofit organizations like The Conservation Fund, Friends of Acadia, Maine Coast Heritage Trust, and other conservation groups. Working together, we can do much more and in a more efficient and timely approach. These groups can, and often do, buy properties that come up for sale and hold them until the national park can obtain congressional appropriations through the Land and Water Conservation Fund. At other times, they use private money to buy and then donate the land to the park.

This wonderful Schoodic story doesn't end there. Soon after the property had closed, the anonymous donor invited me to go with him to look at the property. After the hour's drive to reach the Schoodic Peninsula, we drove to the end of the park road where I had said a new bike path would be needed to cross the peninsula and connect back to the bike ride starting point. As the car slowed to a stop, he said "Okay, where should we put that new bike path?" I thought to myself, this is great. Not only will this critical land be protected, but he is willing to help make that new bike connection. I pointed out a suggested route and also showed it to him on a topographic map of the area.

237

He liked the proposal and then surprised me again by saying, "What else should we do?" leaving me even more amazed and excited. We entered a discussion about possibilities, such as hiking trails, a campground, a small visitor information center, and more. Not being a camper himself, he wasn't sure of the value of a new campground.

A few days after that initial trip to Schoodic, I invited him to tour the existing Acadia campgrounds and pointed out that all 550 campsites were full most summer nights. It was obvious that many families were having fun enjoying the great outdoors. I called it "quality time" enjoying nature without the modern distractions. I even had a poster made up – a collage of photos of smiling kids and families having fun at the campgrounds. They were sitting around a campfire, making s'mores, riding bikes, eating dinner at the picnic table, and even setting up camp, all of which make great memories.

It wasn't long after that initial drive in the park, we began calling the project Schoodic Woods. He designated a project manager who hired a landscape architect and an architect to develop the plan. In close coordination with the National Park Service (me), the small planning group came up with an outstanding plan to provide for increased public use and enjoyment of the soon to be expanded Schoodic District of Acadia. It called for constructing new facilities and ultimately donating everything, including the south half of the newly acquired land, to Acadia National Park. The official park boundary would need to change, but I knew there were several options for accomplishing that important step.

Two years later, U.S. Senator Angus King of Maine and a crowd of enthusiastic community folks dedicated Schoodic Woods as an extraordinary addition to Acadia. The beautifully designed and constructed visitor facilities included a mid-sized campground (94 sites), ranger station/information center, a small maintenance building, 8.5 miles of multiple-use (bike) trails, 4.5 miles of hiking trails, and a day use parking lot. Everything was done to the highest standards and with NPS approval. The best example of these high standards was the undergrounding of the utility line down the main road that would become the new entrance to Schoodic Woods and the Schoodic District. This was no easy task with so much granite near the surface. Crews had to blast away solid rock to create the trench for the new electric lines. Local Winter Harbor residents were glad when the blasting was done, and we were pleased when the longstanding above ground eyesore was gone.

In the philanthropic tradition that originally created Acadia National Park, this anonymous donor acted swiftly and decisively to protect the park from significant degradation. This land and the distinctive new facilities have become a spectacular gift to all Americans. This incredible generosity was another great example of private individuals changing the history of Acadia National Park.

Reflecting on that early morning meeting in the Boston airport reminds me that we never know what can come from a clear set of priorities (protecting the land) and some perseverance (never give up in defense of national parks). In addition, this great outcome resulted from the increased public awareness, effective partnerships, recognizing opportunities as they arise, and being in the right place at the right time.

The new information center at Schoodic Woods.

New campground and multi-use trails were part of the
Schoodic Woods gift to all Americans.

Now some five years later, Schoodic Woods Campground is nearly full all summer, and the facilities are recognized as a national model of campground design and construction. In fact, USA Today named Schoodic Woods as one of the top ten campgrounds in the U.S. Campsites are spread out with plenty of vegetation between sites, and every site has at least one electric outlet to allow campers to recharge electronics. This means that no noisy generators will annoy other campers. The local grocery store, restaurants, and shops are also enjoying economic benefits from the 250 or more campers spending the night near the community each day. At the same time, the scale of the development is not overwhelming the charming towns of Winter Harbor and Prospect Harbor.

A couple of years after the new campground opened, I stopped at the local IGA and I noticed two cars with bikes on bike racks. License plates indicated they were from Vermont and New York which nicely illustrated the potential for increased spending in the community. When I asked the cashier how the summer was going, she said it had been "crazy busy." Another merchant told me his sales were up 25 percent since the campground opened.

— — — — — —

Congress enacts the laws that establish units of the National Park System (except national monuments as I have mentioned), and each specific law that

240

creates a park unit also includes language pertaining to land acquisition for that park. As an example, the law establishing Acadia National Park includes an official boundary map and language that specifies how private land within the boundary *shall* be acquired. The word *shall* is taken as a directive. While this is a legal mandate to acquire those private parcels, or inholdings, it is not always easy to accomplish. Acquisition of parcels today requires a willing seller, then an appraisal to establish fair market value, and finally the funding necessary to complete the purchase. There is always strong competition for land acquisition funding among the 400-plus units of the National Park System.

Often, local officials are not supportive of the federal government buying more land within their jurisdiction because government ownership reduces the tax base. Therefore, there is a loss of tax revenue from these federal properties. This has been a significant concern to many local governments, and one solution has been for Congress to enact a Payment in Lieu of Taxes law. It provides some annual payment to local governments to help offset the loss of local tax revenue when land is purchased by the federal government. Some conservation groups have followed this lead, and therefore, they also provide an annual payment to offset tax loss. Since tax loss is often used as the strongest reason to oppose more conservation land ownership even inside national parks, these offset programs make good politics.

— —— —— —

Through various actions, we have added more than 2,300 acres to the public domain, although Acadia is still one of the nation's smallest national parks in total acreage. Because of Acadia's small size and its complex ownership situation, buying private parcels inside the park boundary is mission critical.

In short, bold and determined action by private individuals and partners clearly resulted in what is now Acadia National Park, one of America's top ten most popular national parks. Acadia National Park, cherished by millions, remains an extraordinary place, thanks to the actions and generosity of many individuals, volunteers, and donors acting in the best interests of present and future generations.

– – – – – –

Earlier in my park career and while at Black Canyon, I became aware of a land speculator who began buying properties inside national parks and wilderness areas. He then either threatened or began construction of incompatible structures to force land management agencies to buy his properties at inflated prices. In one case where the property had no legal access, he had building materials flown into the site to increase the pressure on the U.S. Forest Service. According to local newspapers, he ended up exchanging the isolated piece in designated wilderness for Forest Service land near a ski area, which did not have access problems and was a more valuable property. Based on that success, he increased his efforts to buy other isolated tracts inside parks and protected areas for the same purpose.

One of the parcels he bought was a large piece of undeveloped private land on the rim of the Black Canyon of the Gunnison National Monument in Colorado. The 147-acre piece included the highest point in the park and other highly visible land that, if developed, would spoil the existing wilderness character of the park. After I left Black Canyon for Acadia, the developer built a spec house in 2010. The house, listed for $5.5 million, is 4,750 square feet and is billed as "the only luxury retreat inside an American National Park. From this home with an exclusive address, you will never, for all eternity, see another home or the lights of another home." The slick sales brochure highlights "its location on the rim of the canyon with great views, completely surrounded by the national park, which is permanently dedicated open space." Fortunately, this house is in a lower area and not visible to most people enjoying the national park. The house still has not sold, probably because water must be regularly delivered by truck. Drilling a well would be difficult and expensive because water may be at least 1,000 feet under solid granite.

As superintendent, I was strongly opposed to the developer's plans for a subdivision and the construction of multiple houses in the midst of the primary public use area of Black Canyon. However, in Colorado, landowners can build on thirty-five-acre parcels without local approval. Therefore, I tried to get the U.S. Department of Justice to use the government's right of eminent domain to preserve this important parcel before any construction could begin. I argued that the owner was a willing seller, with only the price in dispute. The owner said the property was worth much more than an appraisal would indicate. I suggested that the court should determine the appropriate value, and therefore, an eminent domain action would produce the best outcome for both sides. When George W. Bush became president, the eminent domain action was halted without progress or conclusion because of a difference in philosophy. Today, political considerations mean that the National Park Service must acquire land from willing sellers only.

As a result, the first of what was likely to be several large houses was built and widely marketed as "one of a kind" residential properties inside a national park. If the existing spec house would have sold at the high asking price, more would have been constructed, adding to the damage. When I left Black Canyon in 2003, this land issue was at a stalemate. No more houses were built, and yet the property was still a major concern based upon the uncertainty of the developer's ownership and intent.

Happily, this became another case where perseverance paid off. Since Roxanne Quimby had purchased and donated numerous parcels of land for Acadia and her proposed new national park in Maine, I told her of the growing acquisition needs in national parks across the country. Building on her deep love of national parks, I suggested she consider buying a few key tracts for other national parks. She expressed interest. The first one I proposed was the remaining undeveloped land at Black Canyon before it could significantly degrade the existing wilderness character of that park. She traveled to Black Canyon to better understand the situation and was quickly convinced of the importance of the 112-acre property.

Roxanne asked me for an estimate of this particular property's value. I told her that since it was a unique situation, a typical market appraisal was unlikely to be valid in this case. Most importantly, there were no good "comparables," a common real estate term referring to other area sales that would be similar to the property in question and used to establish a value when compared to the others already sold. In addition, given that the property was inside a national park, surrounded by protected parkland, in a highly visible location (including the highest point in the park), and within the primary visitor use corridor, I told Roxanne it was "priceless." She agreed, and after a couple of years of tough negotiations, she was able to purchase that critical 112-acre property. Roxanne's dedication and determination literally saved Black Canyon National Park. Without her success, there would most likely have been a number of huge houses as well as roads and street lights inside the primary visitor use area. The vast expanse of wilderness and the high-quality visitor experience would have been permanently degraded. It is now forever protected thanks to her bold action, personal dedication and passion for national parks.

Roxanne went on to buy several more important parcels in other national parks, including Glacier National Park, Colorado National Monument, Saguaro National Park, and Gettysburg National Military Park. She donated these parcels to the National Park Foundation as part of the National Park Service's centennial celebration in 2016. However, her most significant achievement on behalf of national parks was buying more than 85,000 acres along the East Branch of the Penobscot River in northern Maine. Her goal was to make it a unit of the national park system. On August 23, 2016, Roxanne donated 87,563 acres to the United States, and on August 24 President Obama proclaimed the Katahdin Woods and Waters National Monument as authorized by the 1906 Antiquities Act. In addition to the land reportedly valued at $60 million, her Elliotsville Plantation Foundation donated another $20 million for initial development and operations, according to news accounts. Her dedication to the protection of national parks and her great generosity make her one of the icons of American conservation. Many people know of the role John D. Rockefeller Jr. played in acquiring land for Grand Teton, Acadia, Virgin Islands,

Shenandoah, and Great Smoky Mountain national parks, but only a few know of Roxanne's contributions. In time, her legacy of personal actions to protect America's national parks will be widely recognized and appreciated. It has been my great honor to get to know her and work with her to preserve and protect our cherished natural and cultural heritage for this and future generations.

– – – – – –

Park superintendents must never give up fighting to stop or reduce threats to park values and a quality visitor experience, working with local and federal officials to improve park protections, and pursuing every opportunity to eliminate inholdings. When dealing with difficult land acquisition issues, I found it was best to have patience and to take the long view, knowing that a national park is forever.

Threats can be internal or external, and they can come from incompatible uses on adjacent lands or from far away, as in the case of air or water pollution. They can be prevented or mitigated (minimized). The best outcome is to prevent threats by acquiring the threatened land or negotiating some solution that will protect park interests before damage is done. In cases when it is too late to prevent the damage, managers need to work to reduce or minimize the negative impacts that are already occurring.

In conclusion, success at preserving critical land depends on the five P's: Purpose, Persistence, Partners, Philanthropy, and People. *Purpose* is our clear legal mandate or National Park Service mission. *Persistence* speaks for itself – thinking long term and never giving up. *Partners* are nonprofit conservation organizations and land trusts that can help buy and hold key parcels while we line up funding and/or advocate for their protection. *Philanthropy* is looking for opportunities to fund projects with private donations or foundation grants instead of government money. In some cases, private money can be used as a match with government funds. In the end, it is really about *people* because these magnificent places belong to all Americans; they make up *our* collective natural and cultural heritage to be protected and enjoyed for this and future generations.

CHAPTER NINE

DRIVEN BY A PASSION FOR THE MISSION AND PUBLIC SERVICE

S tanding in line to order a sandwich in a downtown deli one summer day, I was in uniform and easily recognizable as a park ranger. In front of me was a cute but bashful little girl of about five or six. She was holding on tight to her mother who said to her, "Go ahead, tell him." The little girl looked at me, then away, and shook her head. The mother said, "Go ahead. Tell him; he would like to know." Finally, she looked up at me with big brown eyes, and in a quiet voice she said: "I'm a junior ranger." She was adorable and proud. I congratulated her and told her how wonderful that was. It was such a neat moment there in the Bar Harbor Subway, a little more inspiration for my life's work.

Proud new junior rangers on top of Cadillac Mountain.

- - - - - -

Despite the fact that Acadia is one of our nation's smallest national parks, it is cherished by the millions of people who visit it each year. Good Morning America viewers named Acadia "America's Favorite Place" in 2014 for good reason. It is packed with great natural and cultural resources for people of all ages to enjoy.

One of the great things about Acadia, or any other national park, is the amazing variety of ways people experience these extraordinary places. On a single day in Acadia, you could encounter:

- A teacher with a class full of kids learning about tides and the importance of the intertidal zone
- An artist painting a landscape as they overlook Acadia's rugged pink granite coast

- Kayakers exploring one of Acadia's offshore islands like Bald Porcupine or Rum Key
- A crowd of bird watchers looking through scopes as an adult peregrine falcon feeds its chicks high above on Champlain Mountain's cliff face
- Volunteers improving drainage along one of Acadia's many popular hiking trails
- The visitor center announcement and introduction of several new junior rangers
- The early morning crowd awaiting sunrise on top of Cadillac Mountain
- Enthusiastic hikers reaching the top of the Precipice or the Beehive full of excitement and energy reflecting their unique experience on these historic iron rung trails
- A large family enjoying stories and s'mores around their campfire at one of the three park campgrounds
- A ranger-led group of folks interested in the summer flowers and unique plants on Little Moose Island
- Or some eager stargazers on a ranger night sky program at Sand Beach

These experiences, and many others, bring a great sense of appreciation for the extraordinary qualities of nature and history exemplified in our national parks.

Thrilled by the power of nature on display at Thunder Hole.

- - - - - -

The biggest challenge facing many park managers is how to deal with growing numbers of visitors and the resulting increase in traffic, parking issues, and corresponding demand for services. This is particularly true in these times of decreasing financial and staffing resources. Since 2010, Rocky Mountain's visits have gone up 55 percent while the budget has gone down 17 percent when adjusted for inflation. Similarly, Acadia visits are also up 55 percent, yet the park budget is down 8 percent. To put the Acadia situation in perspective, the entire seasonal workforce of 150-plus seasonal employees accounts for about 10 percent of the park's budget. Acadia cannot adequately protect park resources and serve the visiting public without seasonal employees. Further budget reductions will likely mean curtailed visitor center hours with some facilities being closed altogether; park ranger-led programs will be dropped or dramatically reduced; emergency response time will increase; resource monitoring and restoration programs will be a distant memory; and restrooms will not be as clean. In short, both the parks and the visitor experience will suffer as a result.

Many parks will allow some permanent positions to remain unfilled (after a transfer or retirement) to fund the critical seasonal positions. Of course, any vacant position means that other work is not being done. As an example, at Rocky Mountain my former position, the deputy superintendent, has been left unfilled, which puts a tremendous extra burden on the superintendent and division chiefs. As we used to say, "doing more with less" quickly leads to "doing less with less." As the budget squeeze gets worse, each year parks are forced to make tradeoffs, such as eliminating lifeguards versus reducing hours at a visitor center, or cleaning restrooms less frequently versus having fewer rangers to provide vital public services. The choices are getting more difficult each year as the relatively small annual decreases accumulate, forcing major reductions in park operations.

With 180 cruise ships coming each year as well as more visitors in general, crowding and traffic are becoming more serious issues.

‒ ‒ ‒ ‒ ‒ ‒

During my twelve years at Acadia, I became increasingly concerned that young people, with their attention focused on their cellphones and tablet devices, would miss out on the wonders of nature and the unique and compelling stories told in each of this country's national parks. Engaging youth in nature became one of my regular personal goals and the park staff and Friends of Acadia agreed that this should be a priority. Friends of Acadia developed a Youth Tech Team of mostly high school students who spent the summer helping us find new ways of attracting youth to national parks and using technology to our advantage. In conjunction with park staff, FOA also developed the Ridge Runners, Family Fun Day, the Summit Stewards, Acadia Quest, Acadia Youth Conservation Corps, and other programs specifically aimed at youth. FOA annually raises private funding to pay for these important programs. A Teacher Ranger Teacher program recruited up to five teachers per year to spend the summer in Acadia and then take their new passion for parks and nature back to the classroom. The widely acclaimed Junior Ranger Program annually recognized over 1,000 young people who completed the work booklet and volunteer requirements to get their junior ranger badge. Together with similar initiatives by numerous other outdoor-oriented organizations, we hope the cumulative impact will benefit this and future generations of youth. These efforts also will help maintain public support for conservation programs and national parks.

Throughout my thirty-eight-year career, I would often spend days off in the park in uniform walking various short trails or moving around to some of the most popular areas to talk to visitors about their experiences. At other times, I would be in the park in civilian clothes so I could observe operations without interruptions. In either case, I would stop to chat with employees and volunteers whenever I had the chance. Visitor surveys consistently show 95 percent satisfaction rates for visitor experience at Acadia and other national parks. It is great that Americans have a strong sense of stewardship for their national parks. Even with millions of visitors, there is little vandalism or littering in parks where I have worked.

- - - - - -

CHAPTER TEN

DRAWING INSPIRATION FROM NATURE

" **M**om, Dad, come quick! This is awesome!" said the young boy looking at a tide pool along the Wonderland Trail in Acadia. "Isn't this the best vacation ever?" said one young girl to her sister after watching sunrise on top of Cadillac Mountain in Acadia. "That was the coolest hike we have ever done!" said a boy to his parents as they completed the Precipice climb in Acadia. Overhearing comments such as these gave me hope that today's kids are as impressed with nature as I was as a child in Ohio. Compared to sitting at home watching television or playing video games with friends, many of the natural and challenging experiences in the national parks are truly inspirational. More importantly, people of all ages are inspired by nature, and I am always thrilled to see families and especially youth get excited about the natural world and their experiences in national parks.

Looking at aquatic life in one of Acadia's ponds.

Personally, I am inspired by sea smoke rising from the ocean in the fall, the roll of the rounded rocks in and out with the tides on Acadia's beaches, the peace and solitude of walking on a wilderness island in Frenchman Bay, the laughter and banter of a family sitting around a campfire, the reaction of a small child as they hold a sea cucumber or other critter for the first time, seeing the riot of fall colors in the trees and ground cover of Acadia in early October, watching a majestic loon shelter its young chicks under its wings, and contemplating how so many people have come to love and support their National Park System. I am truly inspired by many great memories of my years working in and visiting national parks. Here are a few of my favorites:

- Early one spring morning in Rocky Mountain, Barb and I were sitting on a rock at one end of Cub Lake having a snack. We were looking at the intricate honeycomb ice formations on the lake surface when a strong gust of wind pushed the ice down the lake toward us. What a surprise to hear the musical tinkling created by the collapsing honeycombs. It was magical!

- We were all alone and cross-country skiing along the South Rim of the Black Canyon of the Gunnison under a full moon. The wonderful solitude and serenity were made even more special by the multitude of sparkles caused by the moon reflecting off the mica densely sprinkled among the rocks along the canyon rim. It was a "you had to be there" experience once again emphasizing the magic in nature.

- Backpacking from Bear Lake twenty-five miles over Flattop Mountain with my son, camping one night along a mountain stream, before hiking out to Grand Lake and the nearest Dairy Queen for a couple of delicious milkshakes. Simple pleasures and shared family experiences are the best!

- Having the American citizenship ceremony at Jordan Pond in Acadia, and as superintendent, welcoming these new citizens and telling them they are now part owners of Acadia and other national parks.

- Placing sleep pads on the terrace at Rocky's Alpine Visitor Center at nearly 12,000 feet elevation, watching the Perseids meteor shower in the pitch dark and total quiet except for the oohs and aahs of friends and colleagues. Thankfully, dark night skies are still possible in many of our national parks.

- Standing with a small crowd in the trees watching a mother moose and two calves grazing on the bottom of a shallow pond in the Kawuneeche Valley and listening to the excitement in the whispered comments from other visitors.

255

- Being high on Rocky's Trail Ridge Road and having blue sky above and cloud-filled valleys below while handsome bull elk with huge racks grazed the alpine meadows. Enchanting! And then with camera in hand, kneeling to appreciate the alpine wildflowers such as sky pilot, alpine paintbrush, shooting star and forget-me-not. It could not have been more perfect.

- Seeing the still steaming elk calf just born on a cold spring morning while hiking to Spirit Lake in the Rocky Mountains —a spiritual experience indeed. Spring and new life go hand in hand.

- The peace and solitude of snowshoeing up to Dream Lake via Emerald and Nymph Lakes. The deep snow insulates everything protecting the natural quiet. It allows us to appreciate the whisper of the wind and the trickle of water beneath the ice on the cascading stream connecting these high mountain lakes.

- Meeting a family on vacation that is spending one day volunteering on a cleanup to demonstrate to their kids the principle of giving back and common ownership of our great national parks.

- The spectacular view from the top of Mount Ypsilon (13,514 feet) looking down the southeast couloir to Spectacle Lakes 1,500 feet below. We had climbed over 3,000 feet to get to the top and summited both Mount Chapin and Chiquita along the way. Just over eight miles round trip, that was my last hike in Rocky before moving to Black Canyon National Park.

These quiet moments of contemplation and marvel always remind me of the incredible vision of the people who worked to establish the national parks so others can be inspired as I am when enjoying these extraordinary places.

— — — — — —

Hiker enjoying the solitude and tranquility of one of the
many high mountain lakes in Rocky Mountain NP.

CHAPTER ELEVEN

CONCLUSION

Today, the National Park System encompasses over 400 parks, monuments, recreation areas and historic sites representing the natural and cultural heritage of this nation. These are the authentic heirlooms that we want to be sure that others appreciate and enjoy as much as we do. Just as importantly, we want to assure that they are well preserved as our legacy to future generations.

During my wonderful career working in national parks around the country, I was particularly impressed by the dedication and energy of the hundreds of outstanding employees I met along the way. I was equally impressed by the amazing contributions of thousands of volunteers who freely gave their time and talents to help with maintenance projects, search and rescue, education and interpretation, science and resource management projects, and much more. And of course, our nonprofit partner groups such as Friends of Acadia and the Rocky Mountain Conservancy contributed money and labor to help us achieve the mission of the parks.

I have tremendous respect and admiration for the traditional park rangers, the resource managers, the maintenance folks, the educators, and the administrators who share the passion for national parks and who dedicate their lives to protecting them for this and future generations. In addition, no matter their job title, they all see themselves as serving visitors in order to provide a high-quality experience and great memories while protecting these lands for all time.

Thinking back to those family camping trips to Yellowstone and Rocky Mountain when I was a child, I know those powerful experiences and indelible memories shaped my life in many positive ways. Like every young kid, my answer to the question "What do you want to be when you grow up?" changed over time from fireman to doctor to lawyer, but without knowing it at the time, I really wanted to be a park ranger.

I can honestly say that I looked forward to going to work each day, and now I miss the clear sense of purpose and the extraordinary people who worked tirelessly to achieve the mission. As I approached retirement, even complete strangers would offer congratulations and thank me for my years of service in managing national parks. I should have been thanking them for the opportunity to be one of many stewards of this country's crown jewels entrusted to us by the American people. My only complaint is that my thirty-eight years working in the national parks went way too fast.

Working on behalf of the American people, protecting our national parks was an honor and a privilege, and a tremendously rewarding career. Employees, volunteers, partners, and donors share a strong commitment to the mission as the stewards of these magnificent resources that belong to all Americans. Passion runs deep in these people, and they are truly my greatest inspiration.

DEDICATION

I was indeed fortunate to serve with so many extraordinary people who shared a passion for the natural and cultural resources forever protected in America's national parks. As a small token of my esteem and appreciation for these highly dedicated rangers, resource managers, biologists and program managers, I would like to dedicate this book to the following colleagues and their spouses who often provided valuable support and assistance:

Craig Axtell (Kris), Resources Management, Fire Management, Superintendent
Len Bobinchock (Rose), Ranger, Chief Ranger, Deputy Superintendent
Mike Caldwell, Superintendent, Regional Director
Bruce Connery (Judy), Biologist, Wildlife Management
Judy Hazen Connery (Bruce), Resources Management
Lynne Dominy Interpretation Ranger, Chief of Interpretation, Superintendent
Joe Evans (Carolyn), Park Ranger, Chief Ranger
Mike and Joan Furnari, Seasonal Rangers and Naturalists for more than 30 summers
Phil Francis, Administration, Superintendent
Deny Galvin, Engineer, Program Manager, Deputy Director
Larry Gamble (Becky), Land Specialist
Mike Healy (Donna), Park Police, Chief of Park Administration
Steve Iobst (Debbie), Engineer, Chief of Facilities Management
Charlie Jacobi, Recreation Specialist, Program Manager

Keith Johnston (Angie), Engineer, Crew Foreman, Chief of Facilities Management
John Kelly, Ranger, Park Planner, Management Assistant
David MacDonald, Land Conservation Director, Executive Director of Friends of Acadia
Linda McFarland (Boyd), Administration, Contracting
David Manski (Shira) Biologist, Resources Management, Chief of Resources
Rick Nichols (Lynne), Park Ranger, District Ranger
Kurt Oliver (Laurie), Park Ranger, District Ranger
Ken Olson, Executive Director of Friends Acadia, Conservationist
Emily Seger Pagan, Resources Management, Land Specialist
Roxanne Quimby, Business Leader, Philanthropist, Land Conservationist
Richard Rechholtz, Park Ranger, Supervisory Ranger
Dave Roberts (Blanche), Park Ranger, Chief Ranger, Management Assistant
Meg Scheid, Park Ranger, Unit Manager
Mike Soukup (Linda), NPS Chief Scientist
Bob and Linda Thayer, Seasonal Naturalists for more than 30 summers, Park Ranger and Cooperator
Jim Vekasi (Mary), Engineer, Chief of Facilities Management
Karen Wade, Superintendent, Regional Director
Sandy Walter (Seamus), Program Manager, Superintendent, Regional Director
Stuart West, Park Ranger, Chief Ranger, Superintendent
Jock Whitworth (Robin), Interpretation, Unit Manager, Superintendent

All proceeds from the sale of this book will be donated to the Coalition to Protect America's National Parks (www.protectnps.org) a 501c3 charitable organization. Over 1,800 former NPS employees have joined together to be the "voices of experience" and address the many critical issues facing the national parks today. See the website for details.